The Making of
a Life

S

The Making of a Life

So Kip,
Thanks for your
support and Love
Agape!

Dr. J. Gentile Everett

ISBN:	Hardcover	978-1-4628-9140-5
	Softcover	978-1-4628-9141-2
	Ebook	978-1-4628-9142-9

This book was printed in the United States of America.

To order additional copies of this book, contact:
Xlibris Corporation
1-888-795-4274
www.Xlibris.com
Orders@Xlibris.com
101018

Contents

"After listening to Dr. Everett speak tonight, I discovered he is smart enough to be the next President of the United States of America"—Larry Taylor, a Campell Soup Executive's comments after a June 24, 2011 Company banquet.

The Making of a Life

This book does not provide all the answers to life's challenging problems. It's just an idea of how to notice the wonderful people God sends your way to assist you in developing values, problem-solving skills, and how to maintain focus.

Dedicated to all of the Mentors in My Life

And

The Mill Branch Baptist Church Members of Fairmont, North Carolina, my family who was always there for me, especially my only living biological parent Jesse Everett, my friends, godchildren, professional peers, and my wife Joan (Tine) Everett who has been an unshakable rock of love and support and to whom I am eternally indebted, and to all who made me laugh along the way. To all of you, I love always

J. Gentile Everett

Acknowledgements

The list of ministers, pastors and professors who have imparted their wisdom and insight into my life would be way too long to mention individually. So the best way to express my feelings is to say thank you my brothers and sisters in the Lord. I am very sure without these unusually gifted vessels of God, I surely would not have the understanding of God that I now have. These tireless pillars of enlightenment patiently and kindly guided me to know the Holy Other, and gave shape to a mind of chaos that was certainly void of any responsible theology. To these faithful patriarchs of my theological concepts, thank you, and to God be the Glory!

Also, I must thank the special friends God placed in my path because he knew unique people need to associate with unique people who just understood that sometimes men are more appropriately characterized as a mission rather than a mere man. During these more than three decades of ministry, our amazing God has sent unusually loving people who just wanted to help me reach some of the goals they would see me so excited about. Oh how I wish I could repay them for being there for me so many times, even taking my phone calls which could come at any time of the night, and they would entertain whatever crisis I wanted to talk about.

And to my friend, brother, and spiritual sister Bishop Anthony and Pastor Harriet Jinwright, who took me into their lives when I was a very young pastor, single and alone in a large city, still trying to figure out how effective ministry was to be done, and grateful I am for those countless days, nights, and weeks when I would show up at their house in the wee hours of the night to sleep. It was so frequent that the Jinwrights gave me a key so I could come and go at my leisure, and never charge me a dime for neither food nor board. Thank you my brother and sister; your kindness will never be forgotten, because God sent you when I needed real friends, and not once did you guys fail me. I am praying for you both always, and will eternally love, and be in your debt.

I must tell my coach, and friend, Robert "Fuga Boy" Brown, who taught me all the basketball skills I ever developed, and let me tell you, you were the best shooting guard I ever met. It is my humble, but accurate opinion that you possess the best basketball mind in our area. Thanks, "Fuga".

Lastly, I thank my oldest sister, Carolyn, who has never wavered in her love for me, along with my sister Beverly who probably is the greatest academician I know. You have helped me understand Masters and Doctoral work. Also to my baby sister, Kathy, my legal expert, and family comedian with whom I was challenged every day because we grew up together (Lake I am glad that's over, it's John's turn now (smile)). And my brother Jewel, my Godbrothers Kenneth Rothwell, and Ulysses McNeill who always offered and expressed nothing but unconditional love, comedy, and social fulfillment, I am eternally grateful.

Introduction

Life comes at us hard. So many young people of our world are clueless regarding to the events of life that will forever be etched in our minds. We will laugh much, but we surely will cry a lot. We will be mistreated and misunderstood, but amid it all, we continue somehow to live on.

I have often wondered how do you become an adult: not just an adult but an adult who is productive and responsible. I pondered this because from the youth of my teenage years to the days of my thirties, I have gone through much. From being sexually assaulted by senior citizen women, (one of which is written about in Chapter Three) to being stalked by younger females, to being harassed by jealous men (I never did understand why), to my life being threatened a few times, to being blatantly discriminated against, to my phone being illegally bugged, to business and religious people sending women by my office to gather dirt they could use against me (and all of this has been confirmed), to those I thought were my obvious friends for life, only later to discover obvious betrayal and to the many other trials, tribulations, and challenges God has allowed me to continue to live, and make a life while laboring through it all.

Chapter One

The Parental Blessing

There is no such thing as a how to book on parenting. It seems to be a trial and error employment on the part of the parents who struggle to raise children the best that they can. And in the midst of taking their children to the place of maturity, I am sure many parents will admit that along the way, they make many mistakes, and if given the opportunity, they would do many things differently including, perhaps, the idea of either waiting to have children or not having any at all. But given the arduous task of raising them, I believe most would admit that they love what they receive from their children, and rise above the struggles they endure in providing a home and other essentials for them.

Although parents look on their children with a profound sense of pride, enduring love, pain, hurt, and disappointment are episodes that are assured to be present in the drama of raising them. The sacrifices are extraordinary on the part of parents, and they are not limited to just financial spending; it is comprehensive in scope, and many times the sacrifices continue until death separates the parent from the child.

The other part of the equation is the response of the child to the instructions of the parent. As I look back on my childhood, my thinking has changed drastically. Let's think about it. When a child is born, it has no idea of the kind of world into which it are born. Yet they live and enter the earth's scene with the ability to think, see, feel, taste and hear. They are endowed with these senses, and because they have them, they are almost forced to employ them and understand events through them without a clue of knowing how to benefit from them or be burdened by them.

A child has all of this extraordinary power encased in him or her and each power stimulates some type of response in the brain. The child is then almost always called upon to make some sort of judgment from that event or stimulation. Not being a psychoanalyst, I am not sure how much of the brain is utilized at any point of human development, but it is relatively safe to assert that during these early stages of development, much of the brain and cognitive skills are still undeveloped or are not readily embraced by our children.

So parents have the tremendous task of instructing their children while their children simultaneously grapple with understanding the instructions of each moment that seems to cascade across the meadows of their minds brought to them from ideas of what seems right to them. Now let's try to probe into the dynamics of this matter. Parents have no guidebooks apart from what they were either taught, or what they have concluded to be sensible in parenting (all of which can be considered flawed on some level). The child has no reference of anything, while immersed into trying to figure out how he or she can make things work to their mutual advantage, and build an everlasting trend of love and trust in the process.

Wow! That really has to be challenging. It's like both are blind, holding hands and walking into a maze of uncertainty, praying that it will work out for the good. Another interesting component is ascertaining, "from where did these children come?" and "why are parents positioned to instruct them?" First, the Christian faith teaches that all things were made by God. That means our unborn children are already made by God. So even though our reproductive organs are employed in the actual human conception of our children, children are already made even though they enter the world as newborns. And if they were made (it appears at least to this writer) that they had some type of existence before they entered on the world's scene.

Well I am sure you are saying, "there he goes into his theological background" and yes, perhaps you are right. But having the understanding that technically the newborn lived before it was actually born, its entrance into this world really is a transition from where it lived. Infancy is therefore necessary so as to become equipped with the required tools for the success in this life. We can easily accept that the responsibility, care, nurture and instruction belong to parents, but the life of that infant belongs to God. Now parents, what makes you parents? What gives you the authority to lead children? Before answering that question, I would love to digress a little.

Being born in the sixties was an unusual period in rural Black America. We stood amid a nation divided by race and the pressure of being intelligent, cordial and respectable representatives of an oppressed people. This was unmistakably glaring to the children of our community. Making sure that the children in our community understood the importance of that was no small matter. Parenting was not just the responsibility of the biological parent, it was truly a collective effort on the part of a community because the conscious of the community had awakened, and the call made to the cause of racial pride was greater than the senselessness of a combative and contentious child.

So parenting was more of a community's assignment. Because there existed a conscious idea that the tools for success could not just be bought with money, many of the tools had to be provided by a community that was interested in promoting higher values that would, in turn, raise the social and spiritual standards of a people who sought equality in our country. I believe also it seems this fueled the idea of physical discipline that could be administered by any responsible adult. And practiced it was. So we're able to see that the qualifications of a parent went way beyond the ability to produce a child. It was about the social, the spiritual and the consciousness for a better humanity that positioned the adult to be authoritative in the life of a child.

Sometime however, a different idealology would emerge as it relates to raising and disciplining a child, and that would be "I brought you in this world and I will take you out of this world." This was often used in relationship to disciplining a child. This would be used to intimidate or threaten children in our community to conform to the acceptable standard of order. One may consider this primitive or barbaric but sometimes, in many cases, it saved a child from self-destruction. I do concur, if taken literally, and without considering the genre in which it was stated, it could appear to sound sadistic.

But upon wholesome reflection, it only was meant to promote responsibility and success. Another side of the promotion of positive behavior on the part of the biological parent was the idea that their children also represented the quality of instruction the child received from the parent. The bottom line is the parent's authority to instruct was not based solely on conception; it was more about character and having a consciousness of Christ. We all probably understand that conflict and contention will from time to time erupt between the parent and the child. It is almost unavoidable. Both entities provide different ideas about different things and even at different times.

I feel relatively certain that most of our parents would admit that one or more of their children went through periods of rebellion, those times when their children just would not conform nor respect any form of authority. These children wanted to have everything their way. It was as though they appeared to be omniscient. Just all-knowing! This certainly may have been true in many cases but probably not in all cases. What was viewed as rebellion could have been the exercising of the mind.

You surely remember those times when we committed some act only because we could do it. It wasn't about trying to make sense, it was simply done because maybe it hadn't been done before, or that at the moment it just seemed to be the thing to do. You did it because you could. It was that simple. It was important that we all understood that mental exercising is not bad in and of itself. The challenge was to exercise without causing injury to yourself.

My father had professional football opportunities, but fate would have it that he decided not to go but instead raise the family he had. Some of his teammates, and others that he played against went on to play professionally. Many years have passed now, and some of those he knew that went on to play professionally injured themselves into wheelchairs, and permanent injuries for life. I thank God, my father exercised himself without injuring himself. So people please understand that it is healthy to exercise, but it is wiser to exercise without injuring your future. Now I understand parenting is designed to coach us in our exercising to keep us from injuring our lives.

Excessive exercise will almost always cause injury. And some injuries are temporary, while others are permanent. Life is full of all sorts of engagements. Some are positive and good. Others are negative and harmful. I encourage all who read this to evaluate carefully what engagements you exercised so you'll be prepared for the possibilities that are sure to accompany them.

As I return to my parental blessing, I cannot forget the brilliance my mother and father demonstrated in preparing me for the life I would eventually lead. My mother was the quiet lady of elegance who was comfortable being the lady she was. She was careful not to worship her children, while possessing a unique touch of love that spoiled us all. My father was the man of the house, who with great pride gathered and kept the family safe and nurtured while always exposing us to a higher education, never abandoning an acute sense of faith in God. School and church attendance, along with participation were not encouraged, but demanded. I credit my father for his enormous insight in helping me develop into manhood. Whether he was conscious of it or not, whatever moved him to lead me was the greatest thing that happened to me.

My dad was aware of my whereabouts at all times, and made sure I did not have unlimited freedom to roam the streets of a place in Laurinburg called "Across the Creek". He brilliantly went with me virtually everywhere. He was able to achieve this not from his physical presence, but with his shared values with certain other men in the community. My grandfather, the Reverend J.B. Everett, Sr., Dr. Frank H. McDuffie, President of Laurinburg Institute (my alma mater) and deacon in our home church, along with my uncle Colonel William Wilson, all shared the same manhood values as my father.

I would spend countless hours as a young man in these men's homes. Sometimes days and weeks would pass, and the presence of "Reb" my name for my dad, was never ever far away. Within minutes, I would be completely in order at the mere mention of some adult saying, "I'm'a tell Jesse" (my daddy). So, the idea as it appears, was keeping children in environments that continued to reinforce the desired values. I am grateful, because from that structure I learned to be focused on positive behavior.

Another very important blessing I received from sober and spiritual parents was developing an appetite for success. In developing that appetite, one had to also be aware that certain developed behaviors would not be compatible with certain expected results. For an example, to be a good athlete, one had to develop consistent training routines, while at the same time make sure habits that would undermined the highest performance of the body were not developed nor desired. This idea promoted a healthy balance between the body and the mind. This wonderful cooperation, we were told and shown, was essential to the overall success of one's life.

As I now reflect, this whole idea was to convey the notion that simply developing the ability to do something was insufficient without having the acumen or mind to do it well. For example, being great at singing, but constantly destroying the beauty of your vocal instrument by excessive smoking and recreational drug use is a clear example of having the ability without the corresponding acumen to do what is necessary to preserve the beauty, and health of your voice.

My parents, and other significant models, assisted in giving birth to new perspectives about how to deal with a variety of circumstances, without stressing over what was needed to get through that moment. Over and over again, in my mind I hear the voice of my mentor Dr. F.H. McDuffie constantly staying on me about achievement, and not just activity. I was a student-athlete, musician, honor student and pastor of two central North Carolina Baptist Churches at the same time. I was busy every day from the moment I awoke, until the moment I went to bed. I remember vividly my high school days. I attended a private high school, which was also a college prep, and boarding school.

Every Wednesday we were required to wear a school uniform, which consisted of gray slacks, a white shirt, and a dark blue blazer with the Laurinburg Institute seal, dark tie, dark socks, and black shoes. Similarly, the girls' outfit were along the same lines. Well, I thought that was nice, and I looked forward to wearing it every Wednesday. We wore it all day for breakfast, lunch, dinner, and for the evening vesper services that were required for us to attend, without exception.

The vesper services were where the school choir would sing, scriptures and prayers would be offered, and usually one of the local pastors would speak to the student body. This was every Wednesday at 7:00 p.m. And of course, who could forget Mrs. Butler, the sister to the school's President, Dr. McDuffie, who always played on the organ the closing song "Now the Day is Over". But for me the most impressive and moving part of the service was Mrs. S.E.

McDuffie, the school's principal, when she would present her "By the Ways". The profundity and wisdom I saw in them shaped every facet of my life.

There I was every Wednesday going to a brief church service, and I wanted to do like the other student athletes and honor students as well as everybody else; just simply go to the brief service, and say and do nothing. But that never happened. At every Wednesday evening service, there I was in front of the student body, reading, praying, speaking, singing, or playing the piano. Oh how I wanted to be sitting with the other students watching the clock, anticipating an earlier dismissal. But that was not to be. Dr. McDuffie never asked me to do anything. He simply told me what to do. And submitting to his instruction was not a problem, it was a pleasure. I was so in tune with having a meaningful life like his, I thought following his instructions was not only respectful, but essential to achieving the desired goals I had set for myself.

Dr. McDuffie, employing a type of falsetto to his voice, would look at my expression and interpret my perhaps discomfort at always standing in front of the student body, and he would say, "Jesse this is only a few minutes out you your life. Don't worry yourself. Just do what has to be done." Little did I know at the time that either through clairvoyance or a prophecy, he was laying the foundation of a principle that would serve me well in my future endeavors.

The Turning Point

I believe there are special moments in our lives when we are called upon to embrace what will truly define who we are. Perhaps, this is what the sociologists call the "defining moments" of one's life. If we would reflect on the history of our lives, most of us would discover that there was a moment or an event that pierced the consciousness of what we are to do with the time we have left on mother Earth. Mine came as I prepared for my first year in high school. A dream of mine was going to high school and playing varsity basketball.

I worked hard to achieve it, and after having a wonderful year just one year before, Mr. F.H. McDuffie, Jr. was the the head coach of this nationally recognized basketball program, and invited me to attend a basketball camp held during that summer called "Camp Horizon". My dad agreed, and paid for me to go. It was grueling. The workouts were long and hard. It was a week before we even touched the basketball. We just ran and exercised. I thought I was not going to make it. But somehow I did, and at the end of the camp, I was voted MVP (most valuable player). I was happy to receive the recognition, and that created an impetus for me to attend Laurinburg Institute.

Coach McDuffie met with my parents, and they agreed to his scholarship offer and to Laurinburg Institute I was bound. I then had the chance to play with players, and against players from various places around the world, and a new world was opened to me. After battling with many to make the team, I was extremely happy to see my name appear on the final roster of players who had made the team. I worked again to prove to myself that I could play with other guards who learned to play on the playgrounds in New York, Philadelphia, and Washington, D.C. Well after my first year, I received my greatest athletic honor, and that was to be considered a reminder of Sam Jones, the Laurinburg Native, the Boston Celtic great and NBA Hall of Famer that is considered to be one of the 50 greatest basketball players of all time. Sam Jones, Mr. Basketball, from the State of North Carolina was my early idol, and to this very day holds a place in my heart that I will cherish forever. Now here comes the boom!

I was excited about the ensuing year, where I felt we could win the state championship among independent high schools when an unexpected turn of events fell on me like a ton of bricks. I was already in the church, and ministering by this time, but after my first year of high school, God spoke to the conscious of two central North Carolina churches, and led them to extend the call to me to serve them as their pastor. All of this happened within a 10-day period, and on the 11th day, Dr. McDuffie called me into his office and told me that I was a pre-season All-State pick for the ensuing year. I was happy, and yet not thrilled, because I thought a decision would have to be made, and I really didn't like either one of them.

Decision Time

What a strange time in the life of a teenager! I loved sports and competition but there was a tug on my heart. Can I go about my teenage life as though nothing has happened? Is this business as usual? What do I do? If I say no to the pastoring am I saying no to God? If I say no to my parents and my coaches will they be disappointed in me?

Then there was the ubiquitous presence of my grandfather, who I still consider the wisest man I ever knew, who was not vacillating in his position on the issue. He quickly expressed that there was not a dilemma, and reminded me that I was to become a pastor because "the voice of the people is the voice of God". My dad, simply out of sheer respect and love for his father gave into my grandfather's counsel, but was clearly not in total agreement with it. I was still unsure myself. So I arranged the following Saturday morning to meet with Dr. Joy Joseph Johnson, another father in ministry, at his parsonage at the First Baptist Church in Fairmont, North Carolina. Dr. Johnson and I met for a couple of hours, and he reminded me of his recommendation for me to pastor these churches, and to remind me the Lord had called me to preach. Without showing any sign of what I would do, I traveled back to Laurinburg praying to God that he would equip me, and strengthen me as I would stop dribbling the ball to begin digging in the bible. I thought, "God here I come" and "if I ever needed You before I surely do need you now!"

Great parents are skilled, it appears, at making adjustments. And the parents God gave me quickly adjusted to my new life, and became as usual my greatest supporters. My dad told me, "okay you are going to be a minister and that's fine but you will not be an ignorant one! You will go to school because no congregation should have to contend with the messes that come with ignorant leadership!" Well, that was my daddy: blunt, brief, sometimes brutal, but always clear in his position. But now he's as soft as a teddy bear. Time is an amazing thing. It mellows us all. I thank my parents, and honor my only living parent for showing me how to be a man, and the importance of faith in God. Again, thanks Reb, I love you.

An Introduction by a close friend of Dr. Everett, Guest Speaker at a company function.

Dr. Everett's most recent introduction at banquet function near his hometown: "I have the honor and pleasure of introducing the speaker today. We grew up in the same home, but different houses. What made our home so special was that we were all treated equally. The haves and the have-nots were treated the same as well. We played basketball for many years. I played point guard, and Gentile was a shooting guard, and he was a tremendous shooter and any time we needed a bucket we went to Gentile. I would make sure the ball was in his hands. He shot the ball with the best of them. During the years that we played together, we only lost two games: one was a local team that won on a fluke shot. The other game we lost was to a team from Gaston County that had two of the greatest names in basketball history: NBA Hall-of-Famer James Worthy and Eric "Sleepy" Floyd. The other day when I asked him to speak here tonight, he replied, "Well Fox, you caught me at a bad time. I can do it." I immediately smiled because just like the basketball days, I knew we would be in good hands. He would not want me to tell you he was a star basketball player at Laurinburg Institute, and turned down a number of scholarships to Division I schools, or that he even went to A and T, St. Andrews, Wake Forest, Duke Divinity School, and has a doctorate in both Theology and Education. He would not want me to tell you that he has written three books, been on the cover of two national magazines, and has preached across the country. But he would want me to tell you that he is Pastor of Mill Branch Baptist Church, and has been preaching for over three decades. His wife is named Joan Everett, who has stood by his side from day one, and is truly indebted to her for all her love. He would say success is the result of being committed to yourself and a set of higher ideals. And finally, I would like to tell you that we both grew up in a place called "Cross the Creek", and we learned in our home there that if it has been done, it can be done. And if it hasn't been done, we may as well be the first." —by Ulysses McNeil.

Dr. J. G. Everett at 22 years old

Chapter Two

Choosing Academic Models

I've been a Paupal, a Pirate, a Puppet, a Poet a Pawn, and a King. I've been up and down and over and out but I know one thing: Each time I find myself flat on my face, I just get myself up and get back in the race; that's life.

-Frank Sinatra

These words of the late great Frank Sinatra penetrated my psyche, and shaped my perspectives about life anew. They serve as a model for me, and started my stride into adulthood. Although, there were things mentioned in it that I clearly understood, I was not nor would I ever be. But the feelings expressed showed me that through the perils, and pains, just get back up and try again. Never succumb to defeat. These words for me were about modeling myself to keep on struggling, and keep on toiling, because in there is a new birth waiting for the opportunity to live, and transform my life from ordinary to extraordinary.

I was able to see, and accept that education should never be minimized nor taken lightly. We must understand that without an educated society, our world would remain desolate, and ultimately doom would unquestionably engulf our lives. The power of education gives impetus to greater human development, and makes our world more pleasant, more comfortable, and more convenient. That's one of the primary reasons I push education, because there is a relationship between a lack of education and poverty. In short, where one exists there is usually the existence of the other. Statistics have presented to us these relationships for many years and truthfully, we cannot ignore that fact.

Perhaps, the challenging part of this for most of us is finding someone who is educated that excites our minds, and to the extent that we want to invest in ourselves into education. That can be difficult for some because one thing our professionals should seek to do in any field or discipline, is to present themselves as real people with real issues, and to have human struggles like the rest of society. We must remember, and be willing to share defeats, or ill-advised silly decisions, and to some extent our shameful mistakes. Sharing some of our not-so-bright decisions does not belittle our worth; it only connects us to the world we all share. Besides, we are not defined by our history, because new attitudes make new histories all of the time.

Besides the personalities I've already mentioned, there are many others who taught me, and guided me to embrace scholarship over academic mediocrity. Many of these great minds taught me to believe in myself, and stay focused on where I was trying to go. I thought as I entered elementary school that as I listen to instruction, I should also evaluate or study my impression of the teacher offering the instruction. It appeared early to me, if the teacher and I would somehow connect on a humanistic level, and if we could somehow relate to each other then there would not be any behavioral issues, because I would deem it necessary for me to follow the instruction. This could be true even if that teacher asked me to do something that I personally thought it was pointless.

My respect for the teachers was to be greater than any other reason I could think to not follow their instruction. As I think about it, the first teacher to arrest my total respect like that was Mrs. Annie Helen Cureton. She was my third grade teacher, and my first teacher in an integrated school system. I must mention while writing about this period, Brown v. Board of Education went before the Supreme Court in 1954. The court ruled in Brown's favor, striking down separate but equal schools by race. It was nearly 18 years later, or so before our county totally integrated the school system. Talk about delayed justice. I'm sure many who were in school during that time period may have passed away before this delayed justice was manifested. So to them it was not delayed, it was denied.

Anyway, Ms. Cureton was a very young, beautiful teacher fresh out of college when she assumed this teaching post, and trust me she beat me every day, I believe. When I would go to her class, I would prepare myself because I felt like she was going to pinch, or paddle me. As the year went on, I discovered Ms. Cureton had an advantage that I didn't know about. She knew my whole family, and they all loved and respected her. This gave her a total green light to either sting my hands, or heat up my buns. She never seemed to side step any opportunity to do one, or both of them.

The part of the story I have left out to this point was my role in all of this correction. You see, I was from a very Black neighborhood, and we had had a very little interaction with any other race. In fact, we were probably encouraged to stay away from any other race because of the racial tensions that existed throughout the city. But in class it appeared almost by accident that some of our white female students and I would perhaps talk or laugh too much in class. We would never try to disturb the class but Ms. Cureton decided to intervene with all the poise, and professionalism at her disposal. But in the end, it appears, I was the one who got the spanking, as usual.

Her correction, her instruction on the social order of the day, her ability to offer balance in expressing her love for me, and keeping me in check have all served well in helping my become the man I am. For example, during all of the disciplining, she would always buy little tokens of her care for me, and bring them by the house. She brought me a white sweater for my 9th birthday, and I loved it so much. I cried the next year when I had outgrown it, and my mother had me give it away. I had quite an attachment to that sweater not just because I thought it was very nice, but because as a young boy, I thought it was my special connection to Ms. Annie Cureton.

As time moved along, I thought more about what Ms. Cureton was trying to show me, and her efforts certainly prepared me for what was about to happen. I entered the middle grades and became involved in basketball. While certainly fascinated by the game, I saw it as a way to express greater dimensions of one's physical and mental development. So in a few short months, the recreation season started and I was excited about playing. The season for me was a dream year. Our team won the county championship, the regional, the district, but ultimately lost the state Championship in Greensboro, North Carolina. That was our only lost of the year, and after a 25 point average for the season, and a 30 point performance in the county championship game along with signing autographs after the game, I tell you as a young black boy in the 70s, I couldn't have been happier with my life. Ms. Cureton's teachings of balance and focus were starting to surface again in my mind. Because now, I had embraced another interest I wanted to pursue while at the same time, I knew I had to maintain my grades at school. Without that, I clearly understood there would be no fun in my life.

It was during this period when I met and surely grew to appreciate what I had been taught. But what's really interesting is how God continued to help me get to the next place in our life. It was as though God sent another valuable person to influence me as I traveled to new destinations. Because no longer being in elementary school, God knew I needed another model to help me develop into a soon-to-be high school student. So little did I know that the next educational potter would exist right in my home church. This astute, and learned man was named Mr. R.C. Dean. Mr. Dean was the guidance counselor at the I. Ellis Johnson Junior High School, and a deacon in our church. What was so impressive to me about Mr. Dean was his sense of humor, his obvious knowledge about many things and his ability to relate to us young boys. He was funny all of the time, and never pointed to anything with his forefinger. He always used his middle finger with his forefinger underneath it, and we would just laugh until we cried.

The other funny thing to us boys was how he would deliberately put his bottom lip over his top lip when one of us answered a question that was way off point. It was his way of saying you are really wrong, and have no clue what the answer is. Then without reading anything, he would go into his academic bank and withdraw a seemingly confluence of data that was very rationally refined. Day after day, I would say to myself that one day I hope to possess an information bank that would just resemble his. Mr. Dean was a country boy from South Carolina, who became consumed early in his life with education, and was passionate about it.

He was not flashy, nor elegant in his dress. He attired himself each day in the seemingly most common suits, shoes, and a white shirt, usually short sleeved, with his signature almost always in his mouth, and that was his pipe. It was usually burning cherry blend tobacco. He would call me little Everett, probably because my dad and I had the same name, and he had taught my older brother Jewel. The day that my connection with Mr. Dean became apparent way the day I left my coat in his office. By this time, I had become an office assistant the last period of the school day. So I roamed the hallways for an hour and a half before school was dismissed. Wow! Man did I love it. I would look through the glass window of the classroom, and pick at my friends who had to be in class.

Sometimes if one of my friends wanted to get out of class for a few minutes, I would tell them "okay." But remember, I was a business man, and if you could give me a quarter and a milk from lunch, I would get you about ten minutes out of class. It was amazing what young people will do. There was nowhere to go, very little to do, but the thought of just getting out of class for a few minutes seemed to be desired by a lot of us. Mr. Dean called me into his office, and I was scared to death that he had discovered I was getting a few students out of class without permission, added with my little business I had going along with it. But it was not about any of that. My top coat was left in his office and it remained there until the close of the day. There was a hawk blade knife in the coat pocket. The knife belonged to my grandfather, and I had picked it up around the house to work on something but never did. Instead, I put it in my top coat pocket and not wearing that coat often, I simply forgot that it was there. It fell out of my pocket, and Mr. Dean picked it up, and kept it for me until he could speak to me. You see, during this time, anyone who brought a knife of any kind to school was automatically suspended with the potential of expulsion. Mr. Dean said to me, "Little Everett, ordinarily I would'a just turned in this weapon and had a little knucklehead thrown out, but I thought a boy in church with outstanding grades with no behavioral write-ups and very wonderful parents, at least deserves to be reasoned with."

It was with profound gratitude, and humility that I explained what happened, and he saw how troubling the whole matter was to me, maybe because he sensed I didn't want to hear the words of potential death, "I'm a call your daddy Jesse!"

As I grew closer to my life's undertaking and my more and more heightened interest in ministry, God carefully placed in my path another significant figure. His name was Mr. Anzell N. Harrell, Sr. Uncle Anzell was what I called him, because of the closeness of our families, and his brotherly relationship with my father. I spent a lot of time at his home. Anzell Jr. and I were close friends. Although, Uncle Anzell did not teach me a formal class, because he was the assistant principal of the school, he did teach me much about how one should personally present oneself to the public as a professional.

Uncle Anzell was truly a master at dressing up. I'm not sure he would have called it dressing up, because he was magazine clean every day. He had a gift in color coordination, with just elegance and class. I did not get to tell him just how often I watched him every day, just to see what a really nice outfit he would sport that day. Interestingly enough, when I should have been reading, or studying the lesson from class, I would be either gazing through the window, or playing back in my mind the classy suit Uncle Anzell would be modeling. I tell you this was everyday, and it wasn't limited to the business days. He was dapper every day, and every evening I would see him.

I recall one day he called me to his office right after a game we had the night before, and he said, "Gentile, you really played a great game last night, and I was really impressed with not only your points, but the behind-the-back passes you made which showed your court vision." He went on that day to tell me to be very careful, and don't put yourself in the position of being a father anytime soon, because if you use your mind you will have a great future. He thought I was talented in many areas. I discovered a striking similarity between my biological parents, and Uncle Anzell and his wife Aunt June. They all believed in having a well-rounded life.

It was never just about sports, but music and academics, too. I am very appreciative for his encouragement, because he too had the license to straighten me out whenever he deemed it necessary. He too showed his love and care for me. I discovered this one day when he saw me a little upset when another student copied from my paper on a test. The other student was rushing through the test so quickly, that he even copied my name onto his paper. The teacher of that class was new, and tried to allege that I assisted the student in allowing the student to copy my paper. I pleaded with the teacher, and tried my best to explain to the teacher that I was not aware of the student copying my test paper. The teacher didn't believe me and wanted to discipline both of us. I was livid, because I did my best to follow the rules of the teachers (except on occasion when I could get around a rule that I considered not very important) but never in helping anyone cheat on a test. The teacher would not listen to anything I said. She was adamant, and determined that we would stay after school another hour and clean up.

There were a couple of reasons I knew that would be problematic. First, my daddy didn't believe in staying after school, because he believed the school's responsibility ended at the ringing of the last bell for dismissal. I surely didn't want him involved in any disciplinary action on me. Secondly, it meant a teacher/parent conference and my daddy would never be happy to leave his office to come deal with a school matter with me. He felt by this time, I was mature enough to follow appropriate rules. Thirdly, this may have lowered my grades in the class, and I was the Beta Club (Honor Society) President. I would not have been setting a good example. So I was in a mess anyway I looked at it.

What made it particularly unnerving to me was I really was innocent. The teacher took the student and I to Uncle Anzell's office and Unc said to the teacher, "I need to know a couple of things about this incident: Did you see Gentile aiding and assisting this student in cheating?" The teacher replied, "why else would the student copy his name?" Uncle Anzell asked us boys to step out of the office for a minute, and we did, but the office partition did not go all the way up to the top of the ceiling so he felt it was better to speak to the teacher in a kind of loud whisper. But curiosity would not allow me to sit in the chairs some distance away from his office, so I eased up close to the office door so I could listen.

The other student said, "Man, you gone get me in mo trouble." I replied, "Look man, if my daddy has to come out here for this, that's when I'll be in trouble, so if he has to come, at least I'll have some time to get prepared for the hurricane!" When the teacher could not swear that I was clearly helping the other student, and I did not have any history of that sort of behavior, Uncle Anzell said, "Look. You cannot keep Gentile after school nor can you punish him for cheating because you have no grounds for that. Secondly, let's leave this boy's daddy at Rea Magnet Wire because if your case against his son is not completely solid, he will come and bring a hail storm with him". "Besides", Unc said, "I know Gentile, and he's not that kind of a kid."

Unc was the one who conveyed an interesting idea about behavior. He was so elegantly dressed, that his comportment coincided with his attire. I understood that from the way I dress would reflect a lot about how I would feel about myself that day, and if I dressed nicely, I wanted my attitude to reflect the class of my dress. Consequently, my activities of the day were to blend in with my idea of dress. It was amazing, actually, how we are a complete circle. Our inner ideas are visible in our personal presentation and our personal presentation seeks to embrace a corresponding lifestyle. Uncle Anzell's idea of class gave impetus to my seeking to be a man of class just the same.

Academic pursuits, as I saw it, was the constant journey to the refinement of truth. Not just to the discovery of facts, dates and basic conclusions. But for the refinement of truth. God knew I needed academic refinement. The providence of God again showed itself. A stately lady named Ms. Dorothy Stadler was the grammarian who provided me the understanding of the English language. She was truly gifted with great knowledge on the subject. I loved communicating properly, but she carefully guided me to an understanding of writing, spelling, along with how to employ the highest possible standards of grammar, when expressing ideas. Ms. Stadler was also a lady who didn't take any flippancy, or talking back to her once she had given a directive. Ms. Stadler was firm in her classroom, and was completely in charge. Please understand she was as tender to her students as the morning fresh summer breeze, but don't get it twisted. If a student needed help in getting themselves, together Ms. Stadler was truly down for the job. And if standard language proved to be insufficient, she could quickly transition into a more colorful one with emphasis that was unmistakable. Clarity was apparent. An example of her acuity to exercise her flexibility, was present one day she was teaching about the subjunctive mood of the verb "be". One of our students was trying to sleep in class, and she asked him a question, and of course his answer was wrong. But his answer was not just wrong, he was very loud with it. Ms. Stadler said, "You see, you are loud and wrong". He replied, "Oh woman, damn!" She said, "Damn? Well get your damn ass out of here!" She made sure the atmosphere was always conducive for those who had come to learn, and that was extremely important to her.

Academic Models

Well, my list of models surely would be incomplete without mentioning the instructor, and friend who carefully applied polish and thorough refinement to my budding life. His name was Mr. Kermit N. Waddell, a law school graduate from North Carolina Central University in Durham, North Carolina. Kermit became very close to my family, and spent countless evenings at our home, socializing and enjoying the moment. He was the Dean of Students and

Athletic Director. What very few people know it was he who assisted me in vocabulary building and the importance of scholarship. He was exceptionally brilliant with vocabulary beauty, along with great oratorical skills.

He was a rhetoritician in every sense of the word. He was very well groomed and manicured and was never seen without his attire, beard and hair at their immaculate best. He took me to Myrtle Beach to meet with Dr. and Mrs. McDuffie one day, and it was my first trip there. Later, he took me to Charlotte to meet with his uncle, the late Dr. E.E. Waddell, Superintendent of the public schools. He had a particularly high appetite for world-class cars, and an unquestionable taste for opulent living in general. It was Mr. Waddell who inspired, and encouraged me as a student and athlete.

After going into ministry, he even supported me in that. He attended the first revival that I conducted in Southern Pines, and brought me home in his new Mercedes Benz. Kermit was the one who had committed to write recommendations for me to attend the Dapper Dan Basketball Classic, and the McDonald's All-American Camp but never brought discomfort to me when I chose ministry over all else.

By the time I went to college at North Carolina Agricultural and Technical State University to study Economics and Music, I was well advanced in written, and verbal expression largely due to Mr. Waddell's influence. This became so real to so many of my professors, even as a freshman. I gave the invocation, benediction, and sang the solo, "If I Can Help Somebody" at Greensboro Coliseum in front of some 15,000 attendees, while sitting beside and later getting to know, the late great and Honorable Maynard Jackson, Mayor of Atlanta, Georgia. I must attribute my readiness for this opportunity to Mr. Kermit Waddell, who showed me how to benefit from God given talent and skills.

Choosing Academic Models:
Sharing the wisdom of experiences with others
who learn from academic models.

Chapter Three

Be careful. You don't have the time you think you have

"The young become the old, mysteries unfold; It's only a matter of time. Nothing and no one goes unchanged—George Benson

As I was in my early days of high school, I recalled vividly that one of my fellow students sang these lyrics beautifully at one of our many school programs. Normally, when I could go unnoticed, I would casually flip my eyes up to some unoccupied space, and wait for these programs to end. But this day was different. I became arrested by these lyrics, and began to ponder the message I felt was being transmitted through this song. Never before could I seem to imagine myself getting what anyone would call old. You see, when you are 16 years old, you think thirty years old is practically senior citizenship. But without any real focus to which I could point, I was enlightened to the fact that the old was not born old. They became that from once upon a time being young. And the calibration of time when you are in high school seems to be as still, and slow moving as a sleepless night amid the quiet solitude of a rural forest. It just creeps by, and we try to believe that time might move but we will remain young forever.

Well, to all the young people who might read this book, I want to inform you that staying young you will not, and the life you once knew you surely will know no more. The anatomical shapes, the speed of movement, the clarity of vision from peers to personal prosperity will your focus shift, and your circle of friends will all be altered with time. New interests, new ambition, new attachments, and new priorities manifest our lives as we move along the shores of life with time being the independent conductor who waits for no one. I remember putting in a sermon many years later, this idea of time. Time became a living motion when God said, "let there be" in Genesis 1:3. That special moment which probably could not understand itself started to march to the cadence of the drums only heard by itself, and halting had not yet been revealed. Time just marched. Time is without respect of persons, and can never be slowed, nor does it retard because someone seeks to elongate the moment. We all are born in time, and we all die in time. Walking, talking, learning and understanding are associated with time.

Now what's really interesting about time, is that it seems to be recalibrated to speed up after we get out of school, start to work, and of course paying bills. Let me say to the adults who can relate, bills always seem to come faster than the paychecks. Anyway, as we further explore the time in our lives (or the limited amount of it we really have) history, both secular and biblical, provide examples of personalities great, and small running out of this most precious commodity called time.

The patriarch Abraham, presented in the book of Genesis was promised to be a father of many nations, but the lack of time prohibited him from actually seeing it in its full splendor. We are told of the same with Moses, another patriarch of the Jewish and Christian Faith. His amazing ascension to be the great emancipator of Israel directed that nation's course to the Promised Land, and he did accomplish great victories along the way, but he ran out of time and could not experience the joy of reaching it with those whose ancestors he had led. This, as mentioned earlier, holds true with figures of secular history as well.

As a very young minister, I went back in history to study the most significant figure I believe of the twentieth century, and his name was the Reverend Dr. Martin Luther King, Jr. His magnificent life only covered a period of 39 years. Within this very brief life span he had to cover enormous ground to rise to the plateau of the greatness that he would reach. Think about his life for a moment. He was educated, attaining the terminal degree, met and married Mrs. Coretta Scott King, he was father of four children, pastored churches, led mass marches across the country, traveled abroad, wrote books, and speeches that still remain documents of prodigious world-wide acclaim. But when we consider these very unusual recognitions, we must admit he had to be either very conscious of time, an incredible manager of time, or both.

I feel relatively certain when Dr. King was called upon to lead in the Montgomery bus boycott while in his mid-twenties, he probably could not imagine that the time left for him to live would be so brief. If he were here with us today, I firmly believe he would tell us that life, when placed in proper perspective, is like a blur in time. The rises, and the falls are seemingly blended into a moment that fades as quickly as the breath you just took.

But this is what we are left with. As we try to make sense of our lives, when the brevity of it is so apparent, it is not until we understand the scarcity of it that we learn to appreciate it. I had to discover fully that time once lost can never be found again, and time that is void of real value cannot be fully redeemed. We can improve our lives by raising our economic value, but we cannot go back, and erase the time we did not value. The greatest lesson, perhaps, I learned about time is as long as we experience it, we will get older without a choice, but it doesn't mean we grow. We do not choose whether we get older, but we do choose whether or not we will mature and become wiser. This came to me during a period as I struggled to understand what I was to do with my life.

As mentioned earlier, I entered ministry very early in my life, and became pastor while still in high school. As fascinated as I was about this new journey, it came with many pitfalls and many, many moments of pain and agony. This is my first attempt at publishing many of these events. What is fortunate for me now, is that I am able to put all of them in a spiritual perspective, or context that has helped me mature as a minister and man.

To begin with, I thought everybody in the church was holy, saved and bound by a code of conduct that would always be about God first, others second, and self last. How naive is that? The church at the beginning for me was anything but that. The problems I had to contend with were very complex, especially for a very young man who had experienced so little in life. One of my first vivid examples of this came to me one warm Saturday in my little pastor's study. A married woman came in and sat in the barely upholstered chair. I was very curious of what this woman wanted with me. I was 17 years old, and after exchanging courtesies I asked, "What can I do for you?" She began telling me about the very unpleasant marriage she was in and that she was stressed out about what she should do about it. She continued to mention how ugly her husband seemed to her, and that they had nearly grown children. She had been married nearly 20 years but was lost at what she should do. She told me she had prayed, fasted, and grew quieter in her responses to him, and this point nothing had changed. So she asked me, "Pastor, what should I do?" I said very simply, "just quit him!" You see, I gave her advice from the mind of a 17-year-old high school student. In my limited experiences with girls in school and the like, when things were not going well with a girl, I simply would quit that girl. And when anyone wanted another I thought they just went and got one. What was worse than my advice was the fact that this woman took it, and her life went into a downward spiral. What a sad situation for us all it proved to be. This was the wrong thing to offer, and the wrong person to receive and act on it.

Time not being on my side, I continued for many years to give counsel before I knew how to address painful events in the lives of others. After being blamed for the dissolution of that marriage, I wrapped myself in pity, praying for strength to endure the vile commentaries of how I was a disgraceful spectacle. This was simply a matter of taking on more than I was ready for. My mind was misaligned with the call of the moment.

The Quite Storm of Emotional Turbulence

As I reflect now, the most difficult moments in my life are those times when I allowed myself to be managed by an event or a series of events. My immaturity was at its worse when my memory failed in recalling the victories God had allowed me to see. Failing to recall your past victories, will many times, cloud your judgment and nurture unwise decisions. Sometimes the consequences are not pleasant for long periods of time. This became apparent to me after many years of ministry. You see, as a young minister and pastor, I was not always capable of making the right decisions.

Although, I was never publically inappropriate, inwardly I was in many emotional storms. My problem was trying to deal with the negative, the ugly, and the sadistic propaganda that the enemy would unleash against me. I would seemingly listen to the negative news more than the positive and many times, I would allow this untrue, cynical information to cause me to leave some good jobs to pursue others. What is so silly to me now, is that I gave my emotional stamina over to others who were not called to do what God called me to do. For example, once while in college, one fall Saturday night I was at my study at the church working to prepare my sermon for the next morning. It was about 10 p.m, when there was a knock from the outside door. I opened the door, and a young lady entered my study and wanted to socialize. She was seemingly a nice young lady, but I said to her that I was busy, and maybe tomorrow I could speak with you after church. She was not amenable to that suggestion and insisted that she be allowed to stay and visit with me. I considered carefully the fact that the church was in the heart of the neighborhood, and the community was small and everybody knew each other along with each other's cars. I was a young man. She was a little older, but still considered quite young, and I was uncomfortable with this scene. I was hungry, so I firmly explained to her that I was leaving, and thought she should do the same.

Reluctantly, and with a plan she finally agreed. I went to a local burger joint. It was a takeout diner, and as I returned to my car, the same young lady appeared beside me in her car. By this time, I was becoming aggravated by the whole matter, and emphatically asked her to please not follow me. She didn't really respond and I thought maybe I will not go back to the church, but instead, I decided to stop at the park, eat my burger, and think about my sermon for a few minutes. As I took my first bite of the burger, the same young lady showed up again in her car. Within seconds, the city police came up to tell us the park closed at 10:30 p.m. So I responded, "Officer, I'm sorry I'm not from here and I just stopped a moment to eat and think." He said, "It's ok; you must be a preacher since I see your robe hanging in the back." I said, "Yes, sir, I am." We said good night and that was that, or at least that's what I thought.

This was during the time of the scanners. People who seemed bored with themselves would gather around the scanners like many Americans did back in the day when the radio show "Amos & Andy" provided entertainment for the pre-television era. When I got back to school the next evening, one of my close members shared the news of the moment with me, and about me. It appeared, the officer called in our license plate to DMV before he approached our two cars. Both our names were read over the scanner along with our being at the park and the time of night. Wow! For three nights I could not sleep. I felt helpless, because I didn't believe anyone would believe the truth.

So I left college in the middle of the next night, and arrived at the police station around three o'clock in the morning, and asked for a copy of the report of the incident. The officer wrote in the report that the two never left their respective automobiles, but interestingly enough, the hearers of the incident on the scanners only heard what their imaginations, and or life experiences spoke to them. I was very prepared the next Sunday. My sermon was done, and I was armed with the official police report exonerating me of any inappropriate behavior. I was ready. I wanted someone to suggest a meeting so I could get them all straight.

As the infinite wisdom of God would have it, after the word was presented an astonishing hush of the whole matter buried any ideas about what happened with the Rev last week in the park. What none of us knew was what God would bring into our lives after the park incident. I had been aggravated by the insistence of the young lady's pursuits, but as I look back on it, I wish I would have at least been a little more tolerant, and a little more patient, because two weeks later she died in an accident. If only I had known, I certainly would not have been so quick to dismiss her. What was the crime in talking to her a moment that night when I was doing my message? I didn't have to spend the evening with her, but regrettably, I do wish now I would have slowed down a little to at least consider her presence. What seemed like three months of agony was only a brief moment that was waiting to fade into obscurity, and make way for the next crisis.

The inability to recognize time continued to plague my thinking as I even grew in my chosen career. As I mentioned earlier, that my emotions along with my being void of any real understanding of time led me to make changes in my career paths and give up on goals, because I would allow obstacles to become irritants. For example, once while trying to lead a church, I encountered tremendous resistance from two or three other church leaders on a very regular basis. Day after day, meeting after meeting these few men seemed to usually conspire to be the party of "no." Many many years ago on a smaller scale, of course, I came to feel what our first African American President, Barrack Obama, feels sometimes when he makes certain proposals to Congress. I came to the understanding that these men were going to almost always take any road, or position that was antithetical to mine. Well, maybe it was my youthfulness, but I would sometimes deliberately choose the position that did not represent what I wanted, but only to lure them into doing what my truthful idea was. I knew it was maybe not the best way, but is showed me that they were not as much against the idea as they were against either me, or anyone, else who gave birth to good ideas.

The problem was it appeared that they didn't feel in charge if somebody else was able, or even more apt to think. But my mind understood this and my impatience continued to get the best of me. These men were retirees, and nothing else seemed important to them but church and what the pastor was doing. I did live in a parsonage they provided (which I pray never happens to me again). But there I was every day. I was young, single, and still trying desperately to figure out what this thing called life was all about. And every day it seemed I heard, "What is the pastor doing today?" If I entertained any woman, even cousins, that made me a player, and therefore not worthy of ministerial service. If I entertained a male friend especially during the NBA playoffs (because it would more likely be during this period), that made me a homosexual, and that, too, made me unworthy of ministerial service. And lastly, If I had no company no time at all, that meant I was hiding who I really was or clinically delusional, or in lay terms, just plain crazy. I just could not win. The sad part of this is it was not true at all, and nowhere near the feelings of the church at large, or even the other officers, just those few who were vigilant, and consistently staying under my skin. And yes, they were good at it. I really liked the job but the few irritants took jibes at me with such regularity, I placed in my mind the notion that I would seek other places to grow in my career. Some 800 members laid claim to membership there and less than five kept me uneasy about the work. I later left, and assumed another pastorate, and within five years, either through death or physical limitations, they were no longer positioned to negatively impact the work.

Now, I better understand God was only preparing me to do greater things by exposing me to obstacles early so my strength would be greater to endure the ministry that awaited. My advice to young ministers, or younger people who feel trapped in unpleasant professional positions is to be patient. Whatever gets on your nerves is purposeful right now. But be assured God is only molding you for greater divine purposes.

My perhaps most challenging moment of not being aware of time is now a sad story to me: I was spending the night at some of the members' house. It was in the heat of an August night. The fan was providing all of the air that was stirring. This man and woman were senior citizens, brother and sister, and happily opened their home to me. I was very thankful, and they told me to come in whenever I wanted. The door was always unlocked. I thought that was nice. I did not always think about when I would lie down for the evening during this time, so I guess I showed up around one in the morning. I left my keys under the mat of the driver's seat in my car. I left my suitcase in the trunk because it was so late, and I decided I'd get my belongings in the morning.

It was a serene and tranquil evening. I slipped in gym shorts and a tee shirt that I had left there earlier, and I lay in the bed to stare into the night as I awaited the falling of slumber to carry me into a peaceful nap for the night. Well around 2:40 a.m., I felt this very heavy, naked weight lying next to me, trying to kiss my face, and with a raspy baritone voice this lady said, "Come on, Jesse." I completely and quickly awoke and with all my might, I said, "Oh Lord, no!" The lady, large and burly with incredible strength, tugged on me. I started kicking the fan out of the window, and then climbed out of the window headed to my car. She yelled, "It's alright, Jesse. Just think of me as one of dem youn' gurls!" I never looked back to respond but after that bout, I could only think to myself, "think of her as one of those young girls". I am sorry, but I am not gifted with that much imagination.

From this began a year of distance and separation between us. I never went there again, and tried to have no contact with her after that. Some of this distance was from having to contend with her negative commentary about the church, the community, city, the state, country, the world and me. After about a year and a half, she called me to her home. But my feelings about her were still stuck in the wrestling episode. I did not go nor respond. It was the only time in my ministry that I did not even respond to someone who I knew requested my attention. Within two months, she passed away, and I had to preach her funeral.

I felt really bad, because I did not give her the chance to even speak to me after the unpleasant event. Who knows; she may have wanted to clear the air, and make amends. But being so adamant in my position, I would not even give her a chance.

Oh how I wish today it were possible, just to go by, and listen to what she had to say! That's why I now encourage all who read this book to be careful. You don't have the time you think you have.

**Dr. J.G. Everett speaking to a large crowd at
a Coliseum in San Diego, California**

Chapter Four

Wasting Time in the Social Traps

Nearly everyone has been in situations that are easy to enter, but hard to exit. Social traps can be found in individual lives, or they can also be found among our loved ones' lives where we have interjected ourselves. Society will often times place us in situations that begin well and will later turn out to be futile. Conflicts constantly occur because things of personal interest may not be in harmony with life work, school, or family. Social traps offer challenges for us to reconcile our right to pursue our personal satisfaction along with our responsibility for the well-being of all who encumber our lives.

In social traps, people behave contrary to their own self-interests while making what appears to them to be rational decisions at the time. Traps sometimes consist of small, immediate payoffs, but large delayed costs. As a result, an individual involves the behavior of one person rather than a group of people. Individuals head in a direction that later proves to be unpleasant or lethal. It is extremely difficult to back out of this kind of situation. These actions (or the lack of action) prompted by ones own self-interest creates long-term effects that are to almost no one's interest or gain, including one's self.

Often times, young people map out long term plans, and map out short term goals to support these plans. However, these short-term goals are not always aligned with the long-term goal, especially if the short term goals present a lapse in time to complete long term objectives. For example in today's society, many individuals desire to become self-sufficient and independently functioning members of society. I recall the situation of a young mother who recently graduated from high school. She had recently joined the Air Force, had a plan where her child would be supported while she was in basic training, and had contracted with the military to receive free room and board. Much to her dismay, her basic training would occur when her child was having her first birthday. The young mother had an important decision to make.

The young mother decided that she would not miss her child's first birthday, a pleasurable experience, because it was too much of an important event to not be apart of. The mother decided instead to delay her entry to the military, while working to support herself and her child. This decision resulted in consequences that were detrimental to herself and the child. Over the next few months, the mother found employment that would support herself and her child. But with the recession, she was laid off, and jobs became harder and harder to obtain and retain. Several years had passed; then marriage and more children.

It was unfortunate that often simple decisions, with what appears to be short term consequences, can have a long term effect not only in the individual's life but to the ones that are loved and cared for. Unfortunately at some point, it may seem to be impossible to reverse the results of short term goals not aligned with long term goals. This in term will cause difficult, long-lasting results, as in the case with the young woman who had the opportunity to create a better life for herself and her child.

Fitting in to fit in

Some young (and even older) people are pressured into drinking alcohol at parties, or perhaps smoking marijuana, or weed because it is the "in-thing" to do. Note that pleasure comes immediately, and their discomfort, a hangover or the munchies come later! The problem with these illicit activities is that we have great responsibilities while functioning under the influence. Many people are expected to perform in some capacity at church when they are recovering from the effects of these stimulants and depressants while others look on to them to make them feel good about themselves. Some of us are supervisors at work, child care workers, and have full time families. The results of these actions will not allow us to function with a clear mind as God would have us to. But yet we continue to do irreparable and long term harm to our bodies that will have an even graver effect on those who chose to move on to more harmful addictive drugs.

Individuals have also fallen into the social trap of obesity. For example, we are in a society today where we are looking for a quick meal that is delicious, filling and light on our wallets. The downside of this, however, is that younger and younger adults are plagued with problems associated with obesity, high blood pressure, and overall health problems. The short term pleasure of eating a few French Fries can contain up to 44% of your body's fat intake for one day!

We fail to take a moment to go into a grocery store for items that are healthy, economical and will provide long-term consequences of healthy, long-lasting lives. Unfortunately, society has marketed these unhealthy fast food items to individuals as quick, fun, family oriented meals.

Social Traps in Social Situations: Debt

Many people go into debt to own many flashy goods that they know their friends and loved ones would envy. Later, however, these individuals suffer when it is time to make a car payment, house note or Department store bill for items that far extend our means. However, individuals feel good about themselves when other admire a seemingly full lifestyle of "things". But what most don't realize is that many of us fail to invest for the future, put away for colleges or other inheritances, or save for a rainy day so that others can notice our $200 pair of sneakers that cost only pennies to make. We must understand, however, that the long term results of this short term pleasure will later be costly to friends and loved ones who could have benefited from a lapse in judgment to fit in with the in-crowd and the "now" thing to do and wear because of an over exploitment of resources that we have obtained.

If we associate ourselves with the same social group we will find ourselves participating with "them" again. Sadly, people that are practicing similar behaviors do not have other people's well being in mind, just their own. This type of selfishness is one of the big characteristics of being trapped in social situations. If we examine it further, we will discover that no one wants to be around someone who is not actively having fun, no matter how detrimental, with them. On another scale, an error that drives drug addicts to continue using is acceptance by their group. A plan is definitely needed to break this seemingly endless trap.

Time Delay Trap

A time delay trap is the trap that involves proceeding with an action that results in what seems to be a small, yet meaningful reward at the time. When given a choice, most of us would choose immediate gratification over time delay. Recognizing that positive consequences are down the road is a deterrent and therefore minimizes the significance of the desired results if they are not immediate. Someone who has chosen to drop out of high school has been caught in this trap of being an adult too early as opposed to graduating from high school, a decision that will produce more opportunities in the long run.

Time delay in social situations can often seem to be a short-term solution for long term goals. But whenever there are social reinforcements to support decisions that are life-changing, the trap becomes more and more apparent in our lives.

How can we avoid social traps in social situations? How can we eliminate investing precious time, money and emotions into situations that in turn, do not give us back what we need? First, individuals have to learn to set limits on on their involvement in situations, and determine what could be possible outcomes. Set limits on your involvement and commitment. Set a limit and stick to it. And more importantly, do not look to others to always make the important decisions in your life, especially if they are not familiar with your situations.

Oftentimes, we also have a strong desire to impress others. At all cost we must avoid this social trap in social situation. We must remember, however that avoiding one trap does not guarantee you will successfully avoid the next!

Ignorance and the Social Trap

Unfortunately, we oftentimes find ignorance in many facets of our daily lives. Based upon the sheer definition of ignorance, you would think that this would be the easiest trap to avoid in social situations. However, it is quite possible to be ignorant and not know it! Decisions, no matter how big or small, can be based on incomplete or inaccurate information. This produces undesired consequences. Ignorance in social situations is can be present in many aspects of our decision making when we decide to speed in traffic, in our various places of employment, when we are told what "someone said" about us, and other important responsibilities in our lives where we can be ill-informed. A lot of ill-informed, ignorant decision-making occurs everyday but we tend to take it as a part of being natural day-to-day occurrences.

Social Traps in Social Groups

Social groups are not always equipped with the best information to make the best decisions. When there are only a few solutions that are considered, without considering all available information, people fail to consider fully what they have determined and the decisions that were rejected. There are no plans that would contribute to the success of a group in a social situation. By not considering all of the options, the group may sabotage itself, and potentially harm all involved.

Many of us are afraid of failure, change and rejection. In some instances, these fears are unfounded. However, these fears can cause leaders in position of authority to rely too heavily on the wrong kind of information and therefore making the wrong decision for a group of individuals. This social trap involves protecting our egos as opposed to doing what is best for the group. Consequently, we sidestep making decisions that involve high stakes, may hold us responsible for failed decisions, and we look to avoid regret. Instead, doing noting sometimes seem like a safer course of action but in turn limits options and limits effective decision-making.

Dr. J.G. Everett's Automotive business

Chapter Five

Friends Do Matter

Do not be misled: bad company corrupts good character. 1 Corinthians 15:33

People experiencing major life stresses cope better if they have the support of family and friends. Informal networks are the personal ties you have with others.

These networks may include friends, relatives, and other people you turn to for comfort.

Your support system is an excellent way to help you through tough times. In reaching out to others and taking advantage of their friendship, you can receive the strength you need to deal with your problems. Having a support group benefits everyone in many ways:

- Someone listens to your concerns.
- They help you think about options you might not have come up with on your own.
- There is comfort available when you are depressed.
- Financial or material needs can be met.

Your support system may help you through the stress of a personal financial crisis. By reaching out to others and taking advantage of their support and friendship, you can gain strength to deal with your problems and an ability to take control of your situation such as economy to dealing with an unfaithful spouse. There is no lack of things out there to bring you down. Having someone special in your life to talk to is very important for you and your health. Having someone there that truly cares about you and what you are going through, and who are there to help you along the way is crucial to you overcoming whatever obstacle has been placed before you.

Having friends or even very close family members are important. They can lift your spirits if you are feeling down. Just a simple smile can go a long way in getting you back to your old self. There is not much a person can do to change the outcome of certain problems. With the economy, all we can do as individuals is sit back and see what happens. Ultimately, we have no control over that aspect of life.

Dealing with marital issues and family issues is another matter. You can not change many things that lie before you, but you can move ahead and with the help of a good friend or family member you can improve your life. If you have ever been cheated on and think the world is going to end because you lost a mate, then you are wrong. Having a tough love friend to tell you that you are better off and that it was not your fault the relationship ended is a huge help. Having someone to listen to you, and not pamper you, is a wonderful tool. The last thing you need to hear from someone is the "oh, poor baby" speech.

Sick family members, financial issues, a separation or divorce, even a health issue or serious accident: all of these fall under the "in good times or bad" clause of our silent friendship vows. And, it's not always easy to know what to do, or how to help.

Times of crisis effect different people in different ways. Some people reach out for lifelines from their best friends, while others retreat and prefer to be alone. How do you know how to help *your* friend in need?

One thing to remember is that you don't want to give up on your friend. If what they are going through is very serious, it's quite possible that they might push you away or even be in denial. Don't force the issue but *do* let your friend know you are there, unconditionally.

When someone is suffering because of a mistake they have made the last thing they want to hear is your judgments. It really doesn't help the situation at all and, in fact, can make your loved one less likely to come to you for support.

Let's look at an example. Let's say your daughter is in high school and she has just fallen in love with the football quarterback. You think he is a bit of a "player" and you know your daughter is going to end up heart broken. After a few months he cheats on her and she comes home in tears, her heart is broken and life cannot go on. If you decide to say "I told you so" she will never come to you again because she is afraid of being judged. The pain she is going through is a lesson, she doesn't need another one from you.

When people are going through suffering because of mistakes they made it is a bad idea to judge them. Just be there for them and don't inject your values or opinions in the situation unless they ask for them. Ninety-nine percent of the time they won't want to hear them.

When someone is suffering it is really important not to talk about yourself too much. Even if you have been through something similar to what your loved one is going through it is a good idea just to keep quiet. Make sure you just support them. Don't make it about you. Supporting a loved one through a tough time can be extremely difficult. It can be tiring, emotionally draining and sometimes depressing. But it is in these trying times that we learn who our closest friends and family members are. This is where the true bonding occurs and allows us to take our relationships to new heights. The causes of modern social problems, from divorce to homelessness and obesity, are often thought to be based in areas such as poverty, stress or unhappiness. But researchers suggest we are overlooking something crucial: *friendship*. It would appear that our society is ignoring its importance. It is important to have friends that are happy. Happy friends are a powerful indication that your life will be happier, too. Make sure that you play an important role in your friendships. Don't be an outsider. Having happy friends who live less than a mile away was an especially powerful predictor of happiness. It is better to have friends than to be alone. If you are socially engaged, you will have more positive emotions, and you will be happier and healthier! It is important to choose your friends wisely. If we choose friends who are depressed, we are more likely to be depressed. As a friend, you matter, too. You must provide others with the benefit of a friendship by providing happiness support, and just being someone to lean on in a time of crisis. It feels good to help others, and that only adds to your own happiness. A friend is one who believes in you when you have ceased to believe in yourself. Friends are the ones who are always there for you, whether the times are good or bad. They never leave your side, even in the worst of circumstances. When you are sitting with a friend, you don't feel the need to say words. He or she understands even you silence. Still, many people fail to recognize the importance of friends in their lives.

Friends are extremely important in our lives. They can provide a shoulder to lean on. They correct us when we are at fault. They never come into our lives expecting us to change. If you need to hear the truth about yourself, a friend will be there to offer these words by not lying to you, nor will try to please you by simply making you feel better.

A friend is there to count on, especially when help or advice is needed. Friends will be there to offer the best advice possible. A friend's advice will help improve you, and sometimes it may be painful to hear.

Friends should be just as important to you as your family. Friends will do their best to make things alright for you. With friends, deep, dark secrets can be shared without there being a leak in the community. They help us through our toughest pains, and feel happy at our successes whether than our failures. Your friends will never expect anything in return, except for your friendship to them. Friends should make us feel special and should stay true to us throughout our lives.

By practicing our communication skills, our listening skills and engaging socially, we become better people and better companions. With responsibilities at home, having a friend on your side can increase your chances for making dreams a reality. When your friend is there to support you in any of your endeavors (no matter how big or small), this energy leads to one feeling more confident, more secure in themselves and more optimistic about their future. Who wouldn't want to be aligned someone who is progressing in a positive way in their life? Being social with the ones who make us laugh can lead to an increase in positive emotion which in turn may make us healthier. Building a strong network of friends reduces physical signs stress according to many health experts. When one isolates themselves from their friends, they often experience feelings of discomfort, illness or depression.

Has this ever happened to you? You just started seeing someone new and you are crazy about them, but your family isn't thrilled with your new love, so you decide to introduce your new love to your friends. Their response is not receptive of your friend. Our friends are often the voice of reason, and more often than not, our friends are usually right. What you may see as "possessive" they may see as someone who can easily go off. While you may believe that your new friend is an expert on all things, they may feel your new love is controlling and manipulative. Having a differing perspective can often times cause conflict in friendships, but take a hard look at why they are worried. They have your best interest at heart, so take heed of their concerns. Friends are very important. Many people report that they turn first to friends in a crisis. Friends are often nearer than family and can help more quickly in time of trouble. Those without friends suffer from various degrees of isolation and loneliness. In contrast, older adults with close friends spend most of their social lives in activities with these friends. The best friendships usually form between people who share experiences, interests, and values. Friends relax together and receive emotional support from one another. Friends often describe their relationship with words like "love," and "affection". The bonds of friendships are voluntary, enjoyable, and each person is free to make the relationship more or less intense. Certain social factors seem to help determine the type of people who will be friends. Most people have friends who are near their age. Older people may indicate that they don't want to spend all their time around other older people, but when they are around people approximately their own age there is much more social interaction.

J.A. Everett (Tine), wife of Dr. J.G. Everett

Chapter Six

You are Unique. Don't Lower your Personal Standards

Human will is greater than human talent or skill. So dance to the music you hear even if you don't have a partner—J. Gentile Everett

Have you ever asked yourself, who am I, and what relevance do I have on this Earth? This is one of the most essential questions one must ask if they are to truly discover themselves. Self-discovery places oneself in tune with their purpose, which in turn aligns us with the innate power given to us. Another reason why this is important is because so many of us are constantly replicating negative behavior, embracing negative social practices, and vices of the preceding generations, and expecting some new wonderful result.

Too many times, we fail to see the failures of generations before us, and perpetuate the misery of poverty, along with the absence of joy. Over and over again, single parenthood, the lack of education without even the desire of it overtaking many that cannot seem to escape the temptation. So often when the reality of these results are truly manifested, it seems few offspring are able to transcend, but thank God we are given examples, though few, that embrace greater desires for themselves, and with the drive of a sunray, determine themselves to never stop until they get there. Each day I pray that God will change a mind that someone would be enlightened, that ignorance would be no more, and behavior that never produced a positive history would be buried in the graves of time gone by. One of my most passionate commitments is doing my best to keep young people off recreational drugs of any kind. I have seen brilliant minds seemingly permanently damaged as a result of consuming these demons of smoke, sniff, and syringes. It breaks my heart to see it—the paranoia and pain, the lack of organization, and the profound sense of low self-esteem pull us down sometimes even beneath mediocrity. And even after our partnership with these mind-altering demons has ended, so many are left having to deal with the wounds left behind. Certainly, I understand sometimes we get caught up in moments in our lives that do not reflect our truest self, but sometimes the damage done robs us of opportunity and blessings we ordinarily would have had. I know about the religious hyperbole "what is for me, is for me." While certainly there is merit in the statement, we should also ask who does God consider me to be? It does stand to be reasonable, that the definition of yourself will certainly impact what you really are.

I vividly recall growing up in Laurinburg, North Carolina. It's a rural town, with few opportunities for the masses. It was that way then and to many it remains that way. But the lessons I learned in that small town helped shape my views for my later life. What glaringly captures my imagination on a daily basis is constantly being told that you are not to be following the group. You are to be led by your mind and pursue the positive goals you have set for yourself. I see clearer than ever what was really being taught, and that was if you're get in trouble because of having made a bad decision, that's ok. It's okay as long as it was your decision. What compounded the consequences was to be in trouble as a result of following negative behavior acquiescing it in order to be accepted by others.

It is reasonable in many instances to understand God's contempt for Israel particularly in the Old Testament. He (God) was trying to tell them they were unique. They were not to lower their standards and worship idol gods just because it might appear to be convenient. It appears God was saying to whom much is given, much shall be required. In other words, our lives do not have to follow a path that suits the mold someone has fashioned for us. It's not a crime to see your life as a unique journey. It doesn't have to make sense to everyone as long as it impacts the work of God in a positive way, and brings new ways to glorify the Lord. It's well worth the plight, whatever is involved in it.

This leads me into a very controversial religious and social concept. And yes I am a pastor who grew up in a very religious home and was to accept truth as it was handed down without exploring subsequent questions about them. But when we heard about God and the teachings of the church, what did we hear, or better yet what were we supposed to hear? When we become Christians, are we to all fit in a neat sack of dogmas, and to look like every other one who bears that name? Or are we to submit to the Lord, and from that locate our uniqueness and bring great glory to the God of diversity? Diversity in this sense, does not mean ethnicities, sexual orientation, or any handicaps, I'm using diversity to show how God uses many different situations to move us from where we are to where he plans for us to go.

As a young minister, I was guilty of many bad ideas about God and the ways he employs His will. You see, God is bigger than any idea or concept we can imagine. And while in seminary, I recall vividly the day that I learned God was an "Ontological Triune" which means nothing outside of God can judge Him. After becoming armed with this new understanding of God, I discovered that he really could use anything, any person, or any situation to accomplish his divine purposes and does not have to offer anyone any reason why! This is what makes him God over everything. So now, my mind is more open to receive events of our humanity and say that God is still accomplishing His will.

One of the examples of is the story of David, the King of Israel found in the Old Testament regarding this he and his wife, Bathsheba. The story goes something like this: David, one morning, looked through the window of his palace bedroom and saw a young beautiful woman taking a bath, perhaps of purification. He was taken by her obvious beauty, and desired her for himself. He then had her brought to his palace and discovered he had a beautiful passion for her that he could not seem to shake. He had an affair with her, and she later became pregnant. This was very problematic for both of them. First, he was the king, and that was not a positive example for a man in his position. Secondly, she was already married to one of the soldiers in the Israelite army named Uriah. Uriah was in battle during the time when Bathsheba and King David had this affair. When David discovered that Bathsheba was in fact pregnant with his child, he decided to engage in a cover up of his affair with Bathsheba by ordering Uriah to be sent home. David believed since Uriah had been in battle for a period of time, if he were brought home, he would desire relations with his wife.

When Uriah came home, his consciousness concerning his loyalty to the nation would not permit him to engage in pleasure while his fellow soldiers were still in battle. When David discovered that Uriah had not had relations with Bathsheba he summoned him to come to the palace to dine with him. David's intention this time was to serve Uriah wine so much so until intoxication David felt would certainly lead him to have relations with his wife. Uriah was so inebriated that he did not make it home. He fell asleep near the palace door. All of David's plots had failed to this point. David then decided that he would send Uriah back in battle and ordered the captain to place Uriah on the front line where the most fierce part of the battle was going on. Needless to say, Uriah was killed.

David felt like he had been completely exonerated from his lustful passions for Bathsheba because now, Uriah her husband had died. In David's mind, this also paved the way for him to marry Bathsheba and bring her into his palace as his queen. The prophet Nathan knew of what David had done and spoke to David by way of a hypothetical. Nathan presented to David a case that involved a shepard with many sheep and another Shepard with only one sheep. The shepard with many sheep took the sheep that was the only sheep that the other shepard owned, and asked Nathan what should happen to this man? David immediately replied that this man should be put to death for taking the only sheep that shepard has. Nathan looked David in the eye and said to the king, "You are the man!"

David immediately repented and felt the guilt and shame that came with his lewd acts. David was so distraught that when he wrote the 51st Psalms he declared, "Lord take not thy holy sprit from me." David sought to realigned himself with God, and God's punishment to David was the son that Bathsheba was supposed to have did not live.

But as we continued to read about the life of David, he is later characterized as a man after Gods own heart. How can this be when we consider the selfish lewd acts? I now have a new understanding of all of these things. I believed that when I first read this story that it was no way that God would have anything to do with such a person who employs this kind of selfish sinful behavior. Why did the good person which seemed to be Uriah die, and the other two live on?

As a young minister, I only interpreted death as a sign of some punishment. But God was bringing to the culprit of a dastardly deed a new place in Him! For David to get where God wanted him, each act that David committed God used to ultimately get him where he wanted him to be. For the will of God to be completely filled, Uriah was removed and that removal had to be permitted by God. In the end, David continued to conquer other nations. David continued to bring Israel to the top of the world's political systems. God uses people, things, circumstances and even unwilling (or unconverted) vessels to accomplish his will. And as stated earlier, he is an Ontological Triune. Nothing outside of Him can judge Him and He is free to do what He pleases, and is not obligated to provide us reasons why.

This story reveals that our destinies are not determined by the direction of others. Too many times, we fail to see the goodness of God because we limit Him in terms of how He can reveal Himself to us. We have allowed cultural and social idealologies to shape and view our lives and how we see God at work in them. We are able to see in the life of David that although he was not perfect, he had proclivities like any other person. But he allowed us to see that he was an individual, and not an institution. We institutionalize God rather than allow him to be the God of the individual. It's OK to be different, it's ok to be odd, and it's ok to dance to a different beat. God created all of us as unique creatures and each of us is to reveal another dimension, another segment of His glory and being.

**Title: Mill Branch Baptist Church
and Dr. J.G. Everett Ministries 2009.**

Dr. J.G. Everett's 5th anniversary at Elevation Baptist Church, Raleigh, North Carolina in 1992.

The United Voices.

Dr. Everett observes banquet festivities.

Dr. Everett's sermon in Raleigh.
Eighty Six people were inspired to unite with the
church that day.

The J.G. Everett Missionary Choir.

Another Sunday of praising God.

**Dr. Everett offering remarks
at a banquet done in his honor in 1993**

**Mill Branch gives Dr. and Mrs. Everett
a banquet celebrating their pastoral anniversary.**

**Elevation Baptist Church
built under the leadership of Dr. Everett.**

**Dr. Everett's fifth anniversary
banquet in Raleigh, North Carolina.**

Dr. Anthony L. Jinwright speaks at Dr. Everett's
annual anniversary service in Raleigh.

Dr. Everett hosts Dr. Claude Alexander
and the University Park Baptist Church in Charlotte,
North Carolina in 1995.

**Dr. Claude Alexander
at his theologically brilliant best.**

**Dr. Everett addresses
his pastorate in Raleigh.**

The Marvin Ford Inspirational Choir of Mill Branch
Baptist Church, Fairmont, North Carolina.

Dr. Everett
poses with host pastor
Dr. William A. Jones,
president of the
Progressive National
Baptist Convention
in Brooklyn, New York,
in 1986.

Chapter Seven

Getting Older is not an Option.
It's a Consequence of Time

We spend much of our lives trying to deal with the fact that we are getting older. As a leader of a bible study, many months ago, one of our Church leaders whose name is Mrs. Iola Moore said to me, "I woke up one day and accepted the fact that I was getting older and when I accepted that, life became much easier, and I was able to have a much happier life." What that said to me was for us to move, and for us to be comfortable with who we are, there are certain realities we must accept concerning ourselves. But more importantly, we ought to understand that our age does not hinder us. We are still the uniquely designed creature capable of growth, development and achievement at any stage because we were created to do unique things.

For example, the apostle Paul was a trained Pharisee, a religious sect of Judaism that represented the letter of the law of Moses. He was vehemently against the proliferation of Christianity so much so until he accepted being commissioned by the high priest to go and arrest all those who walked in Christ's way in the city of Damascus. We know the story as it is recorded in Acts the Apostle Chapter 9. While Paul was on his way to arrest these new followers of Christ, he had an encounter of the risen Lord and from that moment on, his life was forever changed. He differed from the disciples that had been chosen by Christ because he was led to share the gospel with the Gentile group, a group outside of the Jewish religious system. Initially, Peter and James in particular had questions about the authenticity of his call because they taught that to be a Christian, one had to observe Jewish customs. Paul approach was different. He believed the gospel was so magnificent that no one ethnicity could lay total claims on Christ. What does this say to us? You do not have to be like others to be successful, and to achieve the goals of Christ nor the places God intends for you to go.

When I begin preaching, many around me suggested that I was too young to be ordained. But there was a man named Dr. Joy J. Johnson who said age had nothing to do with growth. It was at his behest that shortly thereafter I was taken before the ministerial counsel to be examined for ordination. What pushed me to seek ordination while being a teenager was that I was driven by what I believed in God, and what I felt God had enabled me to do. I did not believe that I had to be like others. I believed that my uniqueness would allow me to pursue ordination. Even after ordination, within months I became a pastor, and that same idea surfaced again (he's too young to lead). The reason why I felt that it could be done was because my reading of the bible suggested to me that many leaders during biblical times had great responsibilities at very early ages.

I'll revisit the opening quote, "getting older is not an option, it is a consequence of time, but becoming mature is a conscious decision." Neither age nor any preconceived notion play any role in our knowing God. He allows each of us to know him on whatever level we choose because it is a matter of the heart.

Chapter Eight

Satan's Strategies to Defeat God's People

Many sincere and devout Christians walk in defeat. They live a life of struggle, disappointment and frustration. They exist in expectant hope of life in heaven, but miss the joy of a relationship with Christ on earth today because they do not know they are the victims of grand theft. Jesus said, "The thief cometh not but for to steal, kill, and to destroy, but I am come that they might have life and that they might have it more abundantly" (John 10:10). Sadly these believers do not know what their inheritance by faith in Christ really means, and they do not realize that because they are children of God they have enlisted in an army actively engaged in war. Oh yes, these Christians sing the choruses, "Onward Christian soldiers marching as to war, with the cross of Jesus going on before" and "I'm a soldier in the army of the Lord." Yet so many children of God do not understand that these words are more than lyrics to old hymns, they are the battle songs for daily life today.

Sherrer and Garlock (1991) have talked with many Christians about spiritual warfare and many of these faithful disciples of the Lord say that they thought becoming a Christian meant life would be simpler and easier. Others will argue that they didn't "sign up" for battle. These well-meaning believers expected that all their battles were nailed to the cross at Calvary. Still other servants of the Lord will tell you in all honestly, "I never heard of spiritual warfare."

Sherrer and Garlock (1991) contend that many people believe in the devil, "theologically speaking", but their tendency is to think of Satan not as a personality or a being who affects us directly, but simply as a pervasive influence of evil in the world.

How can Christians respond this way? Why don't they know about spiritual warfare? One reason is that, here in America, and in the Western church as a whole, spiritual warfare has not been a part of the regular teaching of many mainstream denominations. In contemporary theological circles, some argue that the devil doesn't exist. It has only been in the last two decades that spiritual warfare has become more acceptable, and some of these denominations dared to begin to teach this topic. Some believers teach that like the five fold ministries described in Ephesians 4:11, "And he gave some apostles, and some prophets, and some evangelists; and some pastors, and some teachers". Spiritual warfare is from an earlier dispensation or is only a minor issue in our modern times.

Others of our Lord's disciples can quote some of the verses related to spiritual warfare, but they do not understand that they must be equipped mentally, emotionally, physically, and spiritually to counter Satan's attacks. Some with dust covered Bibles on the shelf and others, with well-worn Bibles in hand will say, "The battle is not ours, it's the Lord's" as the enemy proceeds to strike them a serious blow. These believers are not attuned to the enemy's strategies, or their role and responsibilities in spiritual battle.

Some Christians suffer unnecessarily because they are unaware that there is a war raging in the spiritual realm and that the battleground extends to the natural world. Christians are soldiers in the army of the Lord, soldiers who need to be prepared and properly equipped in "the whole armor of God" (Ephesians 6:12) so that they may hold up the bloodstained banner of the Lord with confidence, and stand firmly on the frontline. Another phenomenon that also influences the Christian's ability to fight effective spiritual warfare is the occult.

Christians and non-Christians alike are seduced by the allure and beckoning of the supernatural. Interest in the occult has been meteoric and continues to increase. Dr. David Jeremiah (1995) addresses the attempts to legitimize satanic behavior under the deceptive but politically correct nomenclature of "new spirituality" or "new age." He describes how this phenomenon has moved up town. New Age practitioners now wear dark business suits or appropriate business casual attires and schedule appointments at their high-rise office buildings. Well-educated, but Biblically uniformed believers consult with these individuals not knowing the demonic danger they have engaged. God's words to the Hebrews as recorded in Hosea still speak to his people today, "My people are destroyed for lack of knowledge" (Hosea 4:6).

God Would Not Have His Children Perish

But God would not have His children ignorant, and He does not desire that anyone perish (John (3:15) In the last several years, our faithful Father, Whose mercies and compassions are new every morning (Lamentations

3:22-23) has moved through His Holy Spirit, to bring the topic of spiritual warfare to the forefront. God wants His foot soldiers, those in the trenches, to be able to fight the good fight of faith (I Timothy 6:12). As a result of this work of the Holy Spirit, many who were in darkness have come to the knowledge that spiritual warfare is indeed a reality. These believers are learning that spiritual warfare is part of the Christian daily life, and if it is not waged properly, is a major impediment to victorious life in Christ. They are coming to understand the meaning of the Scripture, "for we wrestle not against flesh and blood, but against principalities, against powers, against the rulers of darkness of this world, against spiritual wickedness in high places" (Ephesians 6: 12). Many faithful men and women of God have been the Lord's instruments to lead the way to help equip the church

Neil Anderson and Frank Peretti, for example, have approached this topic differently in their works, but have helped to prepare believers for spiritual warfare with their teachings. Anderson, through his workshops and books, *Victory over the Darkness* and *The Bondage Breaker*, has taught believers to understand their new identity in Christ and the authority that is theirs because of that identity. Anderson offers instruction about how humanity came to be in bondage to Satan, how God provides redemption, and the path that leads to freedom in Christ. He continues his counsel with strategies to help Christians live as "more than conquerors through him that love us" (Romans 8:37). He teaches that as joint-heirs with Christ (Romans 8:17), believers need not live ensnared by Satan. Anderson emphasizes that whom the Lord sets free is free indeed (John 8:36).

Peretti's works, on the other hand are fiction, but *This Present Darkness* and *Piercing the Darkness* have stimulated significant discussions and subsequent studies in the area of spiritual warfare. His novels reveal the reality and intensity of the war waged in the spiritual realm and experienced in the natural realm. They also warn that the enemy's attacks can be blatant or insidious, but can be overcome if believers are or become properly prepared for the battle. In my own teaching on spiritual warfare, I have used these works to help introduce the topic. I have advised readers that although these are works of fiction, as believers in the Lord Jesus Christ they will see the truth that will open their eyes and help them better prepare for the spiritual battles, some of which can have physical, emotional, and mental effects. Anderson, Peretti and others such as Peter Wagner, who have worked extensively to bring spiritual warfare and associated research on the topic to the academic setting, have carved a way to help Christians study spiritual warfare and learn how to put on "the whole armor of God that ye be able to withstand in the evil day, and having done all, to stand" (Ephesians 6:13).

Origins of War

So, why are we, the children of God, involved in this war? Collins and Collins (1996) suggest it is because of God's plan for mankind. God planned to demonstrate what could happen if His creation would trust and obey Him (Evans, 1998). The Collins' *The Shape of the Enemy* contend that one of the angels, Lucifer, "the son of the morning'" Chose to rebel in the reaction to god's plan for humanity. Chose to rebel? Yes, angels are created, spirit and person beings. Personal beings, including humans, have intellect, emotion, and will (Evans, 1998). Collins and Collins (1996) say that Lucifer's pride was threatened, and as Proverb 16:18 cautions, "Pride goeth before destruction, and a haughty spirit before a fall."

Lucifer chose to revolt and declared,

> . . . *I will ascend into heaven; I will exalt my throne above the stars of God; I will sit also upon the mount of the congregation, in the sides of the north: I will ascend above the heights of the clouds: I will be like the most High (Isaiah 14:13-14).*

In these statements, the five "I wills of Satan", Lucifer exerts his volition to:

1. Take over heave, a coup d'etat of the Most High
2. to assume rule over all the angels
3. To manage the kingdom that God had established; "he didn't want to pray, "Thy kingdom come, thy will be done"; he sought his own kingdom;
4. To receive glory. In the Old Testament, clouds are associated with the glory of God. Lucifer wanted the glory;
5. To be like God. Many young people today have joined the chorus, "I want to be like Mike" in reference to Michael Jordan, but Lucifer sought to *be* God. His out of control thinking made him foolish and rebellious.

So it was Lucifer (subsequently know as Satan) and those that followed him were cast out of heaven. They fell out of the original fellowship they had with God with no opportunity to regain it.

Almighty God created man in His image and likeness (Genesis 2:26) and set man upon the earth to have dominion over it (Genesis 2:28). Because of the authority God gave humanity, it would be humans, not Lucifer, who would have the authority that he sought. Similarly, it is man who would be like the Most High because he was created in God's image and likeness. Humanity would achieve what Lucifer desperately desired. God gave man what Satan sought to achieve and announced in Isaiah 14. God established His plan and Satan now works unceasingly to thwart that plan.

Consequences of War

Satan is angry with mankind in general, but believers in particular. After man sinned in Eden, God provided an avenue of redemption through Jesus' death and resurrection. Because God so loved each and every one of us, He sent "His only begotten Son, so that whosoever believeth in him should not perish, but have everlasting life" (John 3:16). Believers, therefore, are a constant reminder to Satan of his future. That future is described in Isaiah 14:15. Yet thou shall be brought down to hell, to the sides of the pit" (KJV). It is a future of eternal separation from fellowship with God.

The curse that resulted from his rebellion "is revealed in the fact that his name changed form Lucifer, the "Son of the morning" to Satan, to reflect his character (Evans, 1998). Satan means "adversary" or "oppose" (Evans, 1998). In addition to a new name, Also according to Evans, Satan also has a new occupation to oppose everyone and everything associated with God. This is how he sets out to claim that which God established and to pursue his goal to "be like God". Evans asserts that he has an agenda, which is to keep the world of unsaved people under his control and render Christians ineffective in spiritual warfare bringing us down to daily defeat. If Satan succeeds in accomplishing any of his agenda, then he boasts of victory, even though it is temporary. His efforts are carefully planned and he will take as many prisoners of war as possible (Evans).

Any person is subject to assault form the enemy; however, Christians represent a "special forces" team that poses a powerful counterattack to the satanic army. Well-equipped Christians can make tremendous strides for the kingdom of God; they can reclaim property stolen from the kingdom. Therefore, there is enmity between believers and Satan. This explains why when individuals become Christians they sometimes encounter a drastic change in their circumstances. They lose or experience trouble in their quality relationships, at work, or their finances. Why? Satan has designated the believer for attack.

How then can Christians engage successfully in this battle with Satan? First, they must understand that in Christ they are "new creatures(s): old things are passed away: behold all things are become new" (2 Corinthians 5: 17). Second, they have a new identity. With this identity come authority and a commission to action (Matthey 28: 18-20). Believers are "joint heirs with Christ" (Romans 8:17) spiritually seated with Him in the heavens (Ephesians 2:6), even though our bodies are on earth. Christians are soldiers in the army of the Lord and as such, must dress for battlefield conditions Believers must "put on (and use) the whole armor of God (so that they) may be able to stand against the wiles of the devil" (Ephesians 6:11).

Satan's wiles are many, but they are not new. They are persistent, but to those who are in Christ, they are annoyances. Scripture calls to remembrance, "We are troubled on every side, yet not distressed, we are perplexed but not in despair, persecuted but not forsaken, cast down but not destroyed" (2 Corinthians 4:8). Satan and his deposed angelic followers are adept at spiritual battle. They employ strategy—long-term efforts, and tactics—short-term efforts to try to overtake this world and humankind. Even though Satan's fate is sealed, he will not surrender. He will do whatever he can to prevent men and women, boys and girls, from coming to saving relationships with God through faith in our Lord, Jesus Christ. He will prey upon every one who names the Name of Christ with vengeance and venom.

The Enemy's War Plan in General: Attack Individuals and Communities

Satan plots against individual believers and the corporate body of Christ. He uses temptation and deception against individuals to try to control their lives, in part, but preferably in total. Collins and Collins (1995) indicate that the enemy builds strongholds (a place of military refuge and a base for attack) in the community and in individual lives. They further identify from 2 Corinthians 10: 4-5, five elements of which strongholds or mindsets, are constructed:

1. Outlooks and philosophies (Colossians 2:8, Romans 12:2)—"arguments, theories, and reasoning" (Amp)
2. Pretensions—"proud and lofty things" (Amp)
3. Misconceptions/preconceptions—"thoughts"
4. Purposes counter to God's will—"purpose" (Amp)
5. Patters of disobedience (2 Corinthians 10:6)

Among individuals, the enemy seeks to control all or part of their lives. If he can succeed with individuals, he makes inroads into their culture and communities, including the community of the church. In the community, Satan seeks to "mould community values in order to create more rebels like himself (Collins, 1995) Within the church he aims to destroy through "mixture", combining the kingdom of God, with the kingdom of this world. Mixture deceives believers so that they straddle the fence, and neither hot nor cold for the Lord. Jesus cautioned against this behavior when He told his followers "you cannot serve two masters" (Matthew 6:24). Satan wages war against the church on multiple fronts because the church is the mechanism for God's plan for redemption. Mixture results in an ineffective church, a body that is distasteful to the Lord. The consequence of this mixture is a society or culture that works for the enemy.

The Enemy's War Plan Is Personal

Spiritual warfare is intense. Its stakes are high, and yet many believers today are unprepared. As a result, individuals and churches are wounded. Evans (1998) teaches that the body of Christ is bleeding as the result of spiritual warfare in at least four areas of life today. These four areas are personal, family, church, and culture. How does Satan attack these areas? In the area of personal impact Dr. Evans emphasizes the effects of the emotions as an inroad for the enemy into the lives of believers. If Satan can seize (the) emotions he can destroy (the believer's) ability to function by crippling him/her emotionally or leading (him/her) into all manner of destructive and addictive behavior (Evans, 1998).

In the arena of the family, Satan continues to cause division and conflict among today's families, just as he did in the very first family. The consequences of his infiltration in the first family continue to permeate the world today. Satan still tries to create disharmony between husbands and wives and parents and children. One of the devil's favorite tactics is rebellion. Husbands and wives rebel against their parents when they fail to love one another as Christ loved each of us (Ephesians 5: 21-29). Children rebel against their parents when they failed to honor and obey them as the Lord instructs. And yes parents rebel when they fail to love their children and disobey the command to "provoke not your children to wrath" (Ephesians 6: 1-4).

The church suffers when believers give away territory to Satan because they are not attuned to the Word of God and cannot recognize false teaching and doctrines that are rapidly and pervasively infiltrating the body of Christ. This is in fulfillment to the warning that in the last days there would be a falling away and people would give way to the "doctrine of demons" (2 Timothy 4:1). Satan will also use the Scriptures inappropriately and out of context to try to sell his wickedness to those who are not grounded in the word of God. Recall that Satan used this tactic with Our Lord following His forty-day sojourn in the wilderness after His baptism. The enemy will aim at any weak point or perceived weakness to try to gain a foothold for attack and thus to divide the body. He will seek to disrupt fellowship, worship, study, praise, and service. In essence, whatever the church does to glorify to God, Satan will work in opposition to destroy it. He many be blatant. He may be subtle. Satan does not concern himself with how he as his cohorts tempts or deceive as long as the result is the believers fail to glorify God.

This cultural impact of spiritual warfare is an area that is relatively new to many in the Western church. Here Satan influences communities, cities, states, and nations to do his bidding. Eastern communities of faith have recognized this tactic for years, but many in the Western church have attributed the Eastern teaching in this to a remnant of their previous pagan influences. However, Scripture teachers that there are demonic forces that have national and cultural assignments. In Daniel 10 the angel of the Lord speaks to Daniel about a prayer request. The angel says that God dispatched him to answer Daniel's prayer as soon as Daniel prayed, but "the prince of the kingdom of Persia" detained the angel in battle for three weeks. Michael, the archangel had to come and assist the angel (Daniel 10:10-15).

The Enemy's Plan Specifically:
Attack Identity, Authority and Action—Get the Mind

Satan attacks Christians' identity, authority, and action in an effort to prevent them from glorifying God. The evil enemy will use whatever methods necessary to achieve his goal. He spares no energy and follows no rules. Satan desires the glory, so he prowls about like a roaring lion "seeking whom he may devour" (I Peter 5:8). Wise (1996) cautions,

> In a figurative sense, Satan likes to ride upon his horse indiscriminately swinging his "*rhomphaia*" sword at the head of Christians. If he can mess up or thinking, he will mess up our behavior and steal glory from God.

In this passage, Wise identifies on of the enemy's key strategies—attack the mind. The "*rhomphaia*" sword was a large double bladed weapon that was used to behead the enemy. Thus, if Satan can control the mind he can spiritually behead believers and influence their behavior because individuals' thought and beliefs direct their behaviors. The same is true for a group or organization, including the church.

Collins and Collins (1996) offer the following insight, "The human mind holds a high priority on the Enemy's program, and this is his main battleground

(2 Corinthians 10:3-5)". They contend similar to Evans (1998) that there are strategic areas that Satan targets for control so that he can blind the mind to the truth of the Gospel. These areas are:

- Political/legislative institutions
- Religious institutions
- Financial Institutions
- The Media
- The Education System
- Science and Philosophy—"intellectualism"

If Satan successfully assaults believer's minds, he can direct their thoughts to paths that God never intended for His precious children to pursue. With successful attacks on the believers' minds, the enemy distort their understanding of their identity in Christ—joint heirs with Christ (Romans 8:17), raised up together, and made to sit together in heavenly places in Christ Jesus (Ephesians 2:6). If the children of God are uncertain of their identity, the consequences are that they will be tentative in the use of the authority God delegated to them.

Consider the authority available to the believer! "And when he had called unto him his twelve disciples, he gave them power against unclean spirits, to cast them out, and to heal all manner of sickness and all manner of disease" (Matthew 10:1). In the Gospel according to John, Our Lord says, "Verily, verily I say unto you, He that believeth on me, the works that I do shall he do also; and greater works than these shall he do . . . And whatsoever ye shall ask in my name, that will I do, that the Father may be glorified in the Son" (John 14: 12-13). Before Jesus returned to heaven he gave this great commission,

> . . . *All power is given unto me in heaven and in earth. Go ye therefore, and teach all nations, baptizing them in the name of the Father and of the Son, and of the Holy Ghost: Teaching them to observe all things whatsoever I have commanded you: and, lo, I am with you always, even to the end of the world. Amen.* (Matthew 28:18-20, KJV).

Jesus has delegated the power that He has to His disciples to continue kingdom building. However, if the devil convinces believers that they are not who God say they are, they will not employ the power that is given to them through the Holy Spirit. This results in bowed down and impotent soldiers. Through infiltration of the mind, Satan can make the believer ineffective for God.

The Battle Escalates

Those who defeat Satan at the entry level, that is, those who enter into right relationship by faith in the Lord Jesus, the Christ will find that he turns up the heat. It has been said that for every level a believer grows in the Lord, there is another devil to attack. Consequently, as believers grow in relationship with the Lord, the attacks escalate and intensify. Satan will assail the mind with doubt, accusations, guilt, depression, and more. He will combat the child of God through emotions with fear, anger, hatred, prejudice, etc. The enemy will come against the believer with sickness in the body, or the mind.

He may also swing at the Christian through work, relationships, and finances. He will use similar tactics against the unbelievers to prevent them from entering relationship with God. Remember the origin of the battle is at the spiritual level. One's spiritual life is not immune from the devil's intrusions. He will distract or induce sleepiness or business so that prayer and Bible study are ineffective and non existent. Satan will try to persuade anyone who will heed him that he isn't as dangerous and deadly as he is.

C. S Lewis in *The Screwtape Letter* warns of Satan's strategies to deceive humankind about who he is. Lewis says that Christians adopt one of two approaches to Satan, they either deny he exists or they see him around every corner. Either extreme fills the devil with delight because the truth is denied. Our Lord says the truth will make us free (John 8:32). Truth will help the believers to live in the fullness of their calling with unspeakable joy—to know Whose they are and the authority that accompanies that identification with Christ.

Satan does not want God's people to walk in their identity—forgiven, though their "sins be as scarlet they are white as snow (they are made) white as snow" victors through Christ—because to do so would mean they would employ their authority. Scripture says that Christians "are more than conquerors through Christ" (Romans 8:37), and "can do all things through Christ" (Philippians 4:13). If believers understood their identify and their authority they would recognize the importance and necessity of putting on the whole armor of God in order to stand against the wiles of the devil—action.

Chapter Nine

Child Development and Christian Education

Child development plays an important role in our society. Leo Leonidas conducted a study several years ago while his wife was pregnant. He had read several articles from psychology journals about the possibility of a fetus being able to hear. When his wife was about 8 months pregnant, he began to talk to the unborn baby. He talked to the baby in their Pilipino language as well as well as the English language. He told his baby that he would be a boy and what his name would be. The doctor said he even put his lips on his wife's belly and called the baby by the name he had chosen for him. The process was continued up until the day his wife was about to deliver. The baby was born on a freezing day; it was January 28, 1973. The baby was born in Bangor, Maine.

The goal of this research was to stimulate the baby's brain development by talking and reading and playing with the baby every time the parents were home. As soon as the baby was born, Dr. Leonidas began to talk to him and called him by his name. Everytime the parents noticed that the baby was alert and wide awake, they talked to him. They spoke to him in English as well as Tagalog. The doctor stated that the first anatomical words that his son uttered was "patella". At two years old Subaru and Toyota were the first two words that the baby was able to read.

The doctor ordered toys that were developmentally at least three months ahead of the baby's age. Mother, father and babysitter stimulated the baby's brain by talking, playing and reading with him on a daily basis. There was also no television during this time.

When LenAl, the baby, went to elementary school he always received top grades and during high school he received only one B and all the rest were A's. He graduated summa cum laude at the University of Maine with a B.S. degree in Biology. He later entered medical school like his father. The parents attribute his successful academic performance to their early stimulation of his brain during his first nine months by frequent talking reading playing with blocks and traveling.

Leonidas' consensus was that people are able to make their infants advanced in emotional, cognitive, and language development by recognizing that the most crucial time of development of a child is from pre-natal to the first nine months of life. The problem with this is that this will only support the top 10 percent of the population because not all people have that kind of knowledge at their disposal let alone the ability to do for their children the way the doctor was able to for his son.

Another expert in the area of child development, Anita Sethi considered herself to be a good post feminist era mom and psychologist who specialized in early education. She did not believe in giving her children gender base stereotypical toys. She stated that she went out of her way to ensure that her son did not play with trucks and her daughter did not play with tutus. Instead, she allowed her daughter to play with trains and her son to play with a doll's crib. She discovered that even with this, her son turned the doll's crib into a car and her daughter became fascinated with shoes. She stated that it took having kids to make her realize that sex differences aren't just the stuff of *Brady Bunch* reruns.

She read and studied many research topics pertaining to 18 month old children that were shown pictures of dolls and cars. The girls naturally chose the dolls and the boys chose the cars. Her research alluded to the fact that at 18 months, children were old enough to have been influenced by stereotypical gifts. The research also suggested that many of the differences seen were evident from birth, and may have been hardwired. What does this really say about gender and babies? This study was reviewed from a scientific perspective. The author reviewed information documented by psychologists from the University of Cambridge in England that studied both males and females. The difference in the gender was starling. There was documented evidence of gross motor skill development, the emotional behavior, as well as a boy's ability to demonstrate at an early age his lack of fear.

The female's study focused on her ability to mimic early facial recognition, early talking and the ability to develop fine motor skills as well as the ability to listen early. The study was from birth to age 12 months for both boys and girls. The study gave a tentative timeline some of the milestones and traits a parent could look forward to as their son aged. This was also indicated for a female as well.

In the study, boys were found to be more adept at keeping track of moving objects. Their gross motor skills do take off; however, during the preschool years, they outpace their female peers in most measures of physical ability.

They are also easily agitated than girls and have a harder time self-soothing. Boys prefer looking at groups of faces rather than individual ones. In fact, given the choice newborn boys would rather look at a mobile than a single face. Lastly, boys were found to express fear later than girls, but less often.

Girls differ in that they excel at imitation. They exceed boys when it comes to fine motor tasks. Girls are more attuned to the sound of human voices and seem to actually prefer the sound to other sounds. They are more likely to establish and maintain eye contact, and are attracted to individual faces—especially women's. They're also more skilled at reading emotional expressions. Lastly, the study found that girls start using gestures like pointing or waving bye-bye earlier than boys.

Science has its spin on what makes one gender different from the other, but in our society, we have women that out perform men and men that excel farther than females. It is what one desires that determine who and what one becomes. This will always be the case.

Paula Spencer, coauthor of *Bright from the start: The simple science-backed way to nurture your child's developing mind from birth to three*, examines the stark differences between boys and girls from birth to the time they begin to enter formal schooling. In the article, parents were discussing the many problems that they face in rearing girls as well as boys. Several researchers explained how female children respond to the discipline and how male children of the same age responded. There was a stark difference in the two. Researchers involved in examining the two genders either had children of their own or had worked with children through some type of family therapy sessions.

Several of the researchers involved in examining these behaviors looked at both genders by examining several areas. These were the different forms of communication, discipline strategies that work for one gender but not necessarily for the other, and lastly their physical safety which examined the ability of allowing each to be willing to take risk and become risk takers which according to the researchers of the topic help build resilience, self-reliance and self confidence. Each topic had both strength and weaknesses.

Which sex is more challenging to raise? Famed gender researcher and psychologist Carol Gilligan, Ph.D., Jenn Berman, a California therapist, Wendy Mogel, Ph.D., and Leonard Sax, M.D., explained to parents the different stages that boys and girls naturally undergo so that parents better understand their children and are then able to adjust their child rearing strategies to help accommodate and nurture their little bundles.

The sample selections came from mothers of males as well as mothers of females. The article does not differentiate between races and the socioeconomic backgrounds of either gender. No specific age was given other than the usage of the terms "birth" and "teens" when addressing the topic of the children.

In addressing questions posed by the parents, there was no discussion of age as it relates to parents so obvious this was not a factor of any significance. This appeared to be an open forum where parents shared their concerns about the development of their children, and the practitioners in this field gave an academic response as it relates to early development.

According to Leonard Sax, M.D., author of *Boys Adrift*, it's also true that each gender's brain and growth unfolds at a different rate, influencing behavior. He also believes parents raise girls and boys differently because girls and boys are so different from birth—their brains aren't wired the same way.

So can we finally answer the great parenting debate over which sex is more challenging to raise? Many psychologists believe like Dr. Sax when it pertains to the topic over which sex is more challenging: much depends on what you're looking at and when. Dr. Stein, Ph.D., a professor of psychology at Virginia State University in Petersburg suggested that not only does environment shape an individual's life but also his or her innate personality helps shape how life unfolds. Parents being the natural, nurturers play a role, too.

There has been much debate over this issue and even with the positive information received as it relates to which gender holds the greatest challenge, this debate has not been settled definitively. This conversation will be held through the ages. It is clear that one should not consider stereotyping the genders because boys and girls are considered by the practitioners equally harder as it relates to child rearing. In examining differences as it relates to the communication of verbal disciplining, it was found that a girls' hearing is more sensitive in the frequency range critical to speech discrimination, and the verbal centers in their brains develop more quickly. That means a girl is likely to respond better to discipline strategies such as praise or warnings whereas boys would not respond positively to this type of discipline. During their preschool years, it was found that boys tend to be less verbal than girls and more impulsive. Boys were found to be more tactile.

It was during the beginning of author Louis Torelli, M.SEd's career in teaching that he realized that the way his classroom was configured had an effect on a number of different dynamics that included how children interacted with one another, how the teacher interacted with the children, and how the staff members worked together. He experimented with the different layouts of his many classrooms during his first six years of teaching toddlers and infants. He reconfigured space and created furniture based on his daily observations. It was at that time that he came to recognize and understand the impact of the physical environment and infant/toddler learning.

The goal of this research was to help well intentioned individuals working in poorly designed environments experience less frustration with children as a result of spending a great deal of time managing them. The teachers spent more time averting problems instead of them developing emotionally supportive relationships with optimal learning experiences for the children.

Directors and teachers in this research recognized how their poorly designed facilities were affecting the quality of care they were providing, so they developed a vision of what type of environment they wanted to create and then worked on a master plan, secured the initial funding, and phased-in the renovations. The future plans were based on a vision that was to be in place.

The new designed facilities helped the teachers to better interact with the development of the students. Many directors envisioned classrooms that were flexible enough to support children's' varying developmental abilities, including children's special needs; therefore, the needs of every child was reached.

My chosen topic speaks to the very core of spiritual and divine purpose as it relates to the Christian Educator. The Christian Educator, unlike his secular counterpart, is motivated by a calling from God rather than the fulfillment of a professional opportunity. This establishes an obvious dichotomy between the two and this distinction will have an immediate as well as lasting impression on the pupils who are taught. The noted Christian Educator and author of "The Christian Teacher" said that

> The ultimate concern will be reflected in and interpenetrate all his professional activities. He not only will understand himself and the meaning of his work as a teacher differently, but his interest in his own discipline his methods of teaching, the way in which he relates himself to students, his view of the life of the college or university community, will all be affected by his Christina vocation which he will try to express in and through his teaching."

Interestingly enough, we discover that teaching is noble as it is takes on a new spiritual dimension when we consider what we are doing. We are responding to a divine call to the classroom. We find the employment of a scholarly pedagogy is appreciated from any school of though; however, the focus and direction the Christian Educator is espousing is one that transcends society; it purposes the students to form a Christian world view that provides him or her with a greater awareness of God, thus a higher order of thinking beyond him or herself.

As a pastor of many years, I have come to recognize that it is not just my ability to speak to an audience, or even be effective in reaching goals as established through strategies and planning. My goals and activities must be geared toward kingdom building, and the hopes of a new quality of life. My undergraduate advisor, Dr. P. Leslie Bullock, was quite careful in relaying to us that paramount to teaching and preaching was that your congregation receives a new quality of existence. As perhaps the greatest twentieth century existential theologian Dr. Buttman would say that what was most important was that each of us experience "an authentic existence."

This seems to be the very foundation of Christian Education. As we teach the various disciplines of academia, we teach them from spiritual to the temporal. Our hope is that through exposing students to God, they discover the wonder of His power and the interrelatedness of Him with the created world.

Further, the Christian Educator does not seek to promote a God divided from the other material taught. On the contrary, the Christian Educator espouses the unity of God with rational thought, and that each discipline is an extension of God, and a revealed truth concerning Him. The idea of a bible thumping ascetic, isolated and/or lowered academic standards are true depictions of Christian schools in general are fallacious and unfounded. The Christian Educator is bound by much higher standards than that of his secular counterparts, because he answers to God, the one who called, instead of a district who simply hired him. The Christian school brings life to education and ushers into the academic process greater clarity of the work and greater understanding of oneself.

The Christian School is a Ministry and a Mission

When we consider the purpose in Christian Education, we must recognize that the very existence of the academy is inextricably linked to God and the greater spiritual good of humanity. Having said this, we must move to that constantly reoccurring question, "Should enrollment be limited to Christian students/families?" First, we must consider who would ask such a question. Would this question come from a community member? Or would it originate from a church Pharisee (if there is a such thing)? The fact of the matter is a Christian School should have as part of its mission to spread the Word of God to all who enter its sacred walls, Shouldn't it? Or can an authentic Christian School really exist on the principles of God and the church and not carry out the Great Commission, in which Christ declares that we are to "go ye into all the world, and teach all nations, baptizing them in the name of the Father, and of the Son, and of the Holy Ghost, teaching them to observe all things whatsoever I have commanded you and lo I am with you until the end of the world".

The crux of the matter as commanded by Christ is to teach all nations. That would suggest that some nations have not submitted to Christ, and perhaps have not subscribed to his teachings. If we are going to deny the matriculation of students who are not Christian, or whose families are not Christian, we could easily find ourselves out of the ministry of Christ. The atmosphere of the Christian Education setting is to assist students in knowing Christ. The idea of allowing students to enter who are not Christians also gives opportunities to the Christian students to witness and minister to them. As I have read and researched this subject, virtually every author in whose material I have studied agree that non-Christian students can be influenced by the Christian students in a very meaningful way.

The impact of this circularity of witnessing, from the teachers, administrators, and fellow students could prove to radically change the life of a young student. Let me quote Dr. Coley in his book when writing about *The Building Block of Developing Unity*. He states, "Nehemiah had the superhuman task of developing a workforce consisting of untrained laborers from every segment of society." Nehemiah third chapter presents an amazing list of a diverse community that rallied to the project: priests, government officials, temple servants, and perfume makers, daughters of noblemen, goldsmiths, and merchants of all types. The techniques that Nehemiah used to create unity among his volunteers were to establish a method of rallying his followers together in times of danger. Then Nehemiah said to the nobles, the officials and the rest of the people, "The work is extensive and spread out, and we are widely separated from each other along the wall. Whenever you hear the sound of the the trumpet, join us there. Our God will fight for us!"

What a testament to the general purpose of Christian Education. It calls for people from all walks of life, those whom our backgrounds differ, are all bound together by a common cause and call. That is the essence of the mission. This is further illustrated by the woman with a poor reputation, but was educated by the Prophet from Galilee at the well. After being educated by the child of God, she became a witness, and emerged a graduate of grief, and began to teach others through her sharing of the gospel. If Jesus would have kept the transforming Gospel, the education of enlightenment, from this woman so many might have been lost forever.

The Administrative Principles

The first administrative principle that we should keep in mind is the way we operate the school, which should reflect our understanding of purpose. As Hebrews states, "Let us fix our eyes on Jesus." The modus operandi of the school will be challenged probably frequently, but as administrators we must stay the course to keep our vessel on course. This too is significant when we craft our curriculum for students. As noted scholar and educator, Dr. Derek Keenan stated with respect to the subject, that curriculum is the planned instructional program that is to be delivered to students. He further contends that the use of textbooks is wonderful but they should not be the last or only resource used in the educational process.

Inasmuch as Christian schools are so closely related with churches, it is suggested that the administrator report to the Senior Pastor who can provide leadership and direction as well as vision that works within the scheme of total ministry. Senior Pastors usually have a very significant role in the establishment and operations of Christian schools so it is vital that they are visible as the school sets out to meet the needs of the students and parents.

Lastly, the primary focus the administration of a Christian school must be to embrace its biblical integration. We can learn about IRS codes, accreditation and teacher certification. Cross-skills, and teaching methods too can be taught by teachers and learned by students, but many of the secular schools could lay claim to do the same or similar things. The difference in Christian educational processes was mentioned in the *Helmsman* by Dr. Coley when he quoted Harro Van Brummelen's book entitled *Steppingstones to Curriculum: A Biblical Path.* The administration of the Christian school must even if it does not excel in athletics or some other extra curricular activity; we always success if we can show them a biblical path.

Chapter Ten

A Scholarly View of How I Saw What I Saw

Nuggets in the nooks: Where do I find what is missing to complete myself? There has to be something missing because I keep assigning myself to new places, new things, and new people. This pilgrimage is filled with uncertainty that is decorated with the ornaments of surprise, so much so until on the surface of my life, there seems to be no pathway for me to capture my dreams. Sometimes they appear to be imminent, while at the same time they seem so far away. Anyway my dreams are usually inspired by the perceived achievement of others and consequently, my dream is not mine completely because admitted or not, our dreams are extensions of what someone else either has done, or defined.

Let's not however, denigrate our personal pursuits to a copycat syndrome. The process for achievement is still good as we engage the evolutionary process towards perfection. For example, Henry Ford, the great automotive mogul, did not invent the wheel, nor the concept of a vehicular cabin, but in finding what is missing, he aligned himself with a known concept and moved that concept towards his idea of personal transportation. In the study of the basketball superstar Michael Jordan and believe me his is truly a study (I say that because during one of the most difficult periods of my life) I immersed myself into a new discipline. And as I reflect now, if it needed a label, it would be called Jordanology. For years, I tediously and laboriously taped every Bulls game that was televised from 1996 to 1998.

During this period of time, I grappled with finding answers to life's questions, and trying to find ways to win in the game of life. I saw MJ win time after time after time. His athletic gifts were ostensibly enormous, and so many before him were given athletic talent, there seemed to be another quality that he had. It was not in his speed, his shooting touch, or his jumping ability.

It was abstract but took on qualities of tangibility. It was untouchable, but it touched every one on the court. What was it? How can it be communicated or explained? Then an epiphany emerged out of my state of mental fogginess, and I discovered it was his will that was greater than his skill. And a new quest to move towards completion immense in my soul.

The experience and realization of discovery along with finally capturing that elusive missing element were not apprehended without an enormous price. Once should be aware that to find is to lose, and the measure to which you find is often commensurate with the sacrifice you are willing to make. What's interesting now is the component that stands between sacrifice and success. Success is not an accident, nor is it a surprise, but it is rather expected from those who want it the most. When one endures insult and injury, pain and pressure, only to rise to new plateaus of success, we treasure it, but make no mistake, we still expected it.

We practice acceptance speeches. We rehearse our walks to the podiums and sometimes refined our public mannerisms, because what some would call egocentricity, or arrogance, the achiever calls expectations. What we all must ponder as we proceed down the pathway of discovery, succinctly stated, is if the price worth the pain. That is the question that must be answered that we must obtain the level of discovery that completes our being. I submit it is sheer human artistry to find the right brushes, dipped in the right colors and shades to outwardly create what we inwardly conceptualize. Many spend an entire lifetime with futile and and fruitless results, and others effortlessly seem to find the right mix and early find the will to pursue it.

They seem unparsed by the prodigious obstacles. They and they alone are the only ones who hear the music of their names designating through the instruments on the stages that are sill in their respective cases and though no human lips are attached, making sound not only impossible but unimaginable. There still seems to be a melody in them that rings out in the arena. And what convinces them that they hear it is the idea that this sound about me is symphonic but not cacophonous. It is a nice vibe and never vile.

Now let's allow relaxation to travel only for a moment through the vast tunnels of our our soul. And as this feeling of tranquility evokes a spirit of calm, we prepare ourselves for the real question: Is it personal, poignant, and pivotal if we are to arrive at the part of peace? That question, though ignored, is never insignificant. What in the world could this question be, you asked? Well, Mr. or Mrs. Curiosity, we all need to know to what music we dance? What chords do you hear in your melodic requiem? Does this tune nostalgically move you or does it transport you into some unexplained soliloquy?

Whatever it does, we are called to listen to our inner music. The dance we will do in life will jibe with the melody we hear in our mind. The music is there, the orchestra is flawlessly directed by the conductor of the universe. Each composition that is played was carefully structured with dynamics unique to each personal audience. There are crescendos, staccatos, and rich flowing legatos representing various stages each will experience if they listen. Let's be clear; your music is for you, composed and performed for you. No on else may be invited to the rehearsal, they may not know why you move to the music unheard and snap your fingers to rhythm that are out of their listening range. But just remember they will hear what you already heard when the concert is ready to be presented to the world. The public should not be privy to rehearsal because that would undermine the shock of jaw-dropping awe that adds to the production of God's show.

The God Show in our lives most frequently come with an odd and much misinterpretation. The awesome God of the universe when ready will raise the curtain of blessed scenes after they are properly and strategically ordered in their respective places in anticipation of that moment, when the firmament of his handiwork were completed with the task of making sure that propitious moment when curtain time, however long anticipated, the right scene would emerge with the accentuated lights, illuminating the points of interests and thereby energizing the elements that are to be emphasized. The tragedy with this gathering of events is the idea that somehow this God Show of blessings is the result of some cosmic accident that created some idea of compensation to those who benefited. Unbeknownst to our critics is the constant reminder that had it not been for the Lord on our side what appeared to be a cosmic accident would have actually been a catastrophic incident.

To further exacerbate what is already flawed, when we walk in to these extraordinary moments of blissful blessing our critics again look to some pejorative term to diminish the greatness of God's Power in our lives by stigmatizing His children or arrogant, persnickety, and socially elites when actually these terms to not come close to describing the person we have become, nor the God who was gracious enough to not allow to succumb to hells that will never be hallowed, nor depths that will never be dignified.

My Child, be encouraged. He says, "No weapon formed against me will prosper." Not now, not here, not ever. Who my beloved of the faith should reject such an unusual display of love? What must be grasped above all else is not the exciting splendor of blessed events, but the almost countless number of unpleasant experiences that did not happen. Oh how marvelous it is to bask in the laurels of success. But the real blessing is to continue to live and not experience the deserved backlash from the transgressions that never emerged in the public rumor mill.

I often find it so amazing when I hear so many harshly react and respond to gossip that has surfaced around their lives. Isn't that amazing? We become irate and indignant, armed and prepared for conniptions that are intended to serve as a prelude to physical altercation, and all of this energy is fueled by innuendo and speculation orchestrated by the minds of the propagandistic. Yet, we are gearing up to protect our character that was eviscerated long ago by the acts we covered well. God, through the infinitude of mercy chose to seemingly say I'll help you keep this one because one more publicized event that reveals what we know just may be socially impossible for you to be taken seriously as a Christian at any point in your life time. Thank God he protected our real shame!

The God Show again is our only way to invite others to experience Him. It must be said over again: It's certainly not about me, but about He and He alone.

Perhaps that's what has happened to us. I say perhaps because bringing judgment to our society is not the objective of this writer. But though-provoking inquiry into the possibly of political and religious leadership caught in the maze of "egomania" had diseased many a would-be noble leader. When all is considered, is it not wise to probe into the super intelligence of the "who and why" rather than the "puffed up, pseudo-intelligence of the "when and where"?

The Super-Intelligent "who" when actually identified can be captured in the words of the song, "Who made the mountains, who made the trees; who mad the rivers follow to the sea, and who hung the moon in the starry sky, somebody bigger than you and I". The discovery of "why" is both existential and philosophical. It is Existential because for reasons to have relevance and purpose it must be linked to our being. Otherwise, it may have cosmic vitality but lack any human value. Further, it is philosophical because "why" attempts to give purpose and pragmatics to the link of something which has to be proliferation of a more enriched humanity.

Who and why are joined to move humanity closer to the plateau of perfection?. Though reaching it seems to most a futile or elusive reality, it is quite necessary to embark on the journey. The journey shows us that human development is the road to enlightenment, and enlightenment serves our cause as we prepare to face the Eternal One. It is tragic to exist outside this realm of though because being caught treading through the uncertainties of life without recognizing that in all things there is a culminating moment of reckoning. That means that throughout our lives we must live to know (or be enlightened) and live aligned with the only real super-power for lack of a better term.

The Great Creator (our God) means for the created to live or I doubt he would have bothered to tinkle with the created at all. But to live does not mean that death is life's great opposition or life's nemeses. Death, when properly appropriated is actually the friend that life did not know she had. When death is understood, he is not a stranger but really the host to God's halos and not the hole of hell. Simply stated, the "when and where" of life takes on new dimensions of understanding when we are attuned by faith to the anticipated results. The "when" of the self-serving, self-centered life addresses or supports the notion that nothing of significance happened until I arrived.

The idea of progressive, positive significance took place "when" I started onto this stage and took the ornaments of nothing and transformed them into opportunities. Notice the almost insurable relationship that exist between "when and where"!." When" again being associated with "I" and "where" represents the place where "I" showed up and decided where my "when" would shed light on my "I". In other words, the "when" is the location of where "I" decided to work, and it did not happen earlier but happened when I got there. Oh how sad it is to be caught outside of a sober understanding of oneself!

The Priority

Our lives are so interesting. The many varied interests and values are woven together to give our lives meaning and purpose. Every life, however, shares commonalities that reflect our species, but pursuing and preserving those commonalities are as unique as our opinions about what we should wear from day to day. We all want to live, we all want to enjoy ourselves while we live. To live for most of us is to have no deadline with respect to our lifespan. No one really wants to imagine a future without being present in it.

Of course, there are suicide missions that perhaps incite the soldier to believe that their ostensible earthly death will accomplish at least two extraordinary purposes, one for the unleashing of celestial omnipotence, or some euphoric carnal entanglement that is more wonderful than the imprisoned humankind can conceive. Secondly, this heroic act or self-sacrifice (which really is self-murder) is going to give accelerated impetus to some enormously needed political or social reform that will usher in a new world order for loved ones left behind.

In either event, the future when envisioned might not include us in the way we currently understand ourselves, it nonetheless does not have us eviscerated all together. We are still somehow linked to a future of some sort. Next, our human curiosities are most uncomfortable when they cannot be satisfied. This is so interesting to me, the power of the reversal. It seems because we do not know, our need to know is intensified. It seems to me in many cases either tell it in totality, or permit it without equivocation and the vigor to pursue the interest in the endeavor dwindles.

On the other hand, to make it taboo, or impermissible is to create an insatiable desire for it. This too is essential with the need to know. We want to know so badly that we will go and drive across town to hear an expansion or embellishment of a told event. We will go further to hear a salacious or sullied depiction of an event of interest. Let's face it: we just want to know. Even if an action or actions towards it is neither welcomed nor desired, and our position to impact the story is so insignificant that whether we know or not anybody cares, still we cannot seem to abandon the desire and interest to know.

Perhaps our unrelenting interest to know has to do with understanding our attachment with the society at-large or with the "what's up" in particular knowing the stories around us places us in some framework regarding our own identities. Each of us in some way affixed to all of us. The Saved is affixed to the Unsaved, the Learned to the Unlearned, and the Haves to the Have Nots. Those who are able via clairvoyance to bring the eschatological into the existential are just as affixed to geriatric behaves like the pre-adolescent.

We are joined together in order that understanding of social, intellectual, and economic segments might clearly be identified. These segments present to aspirant choices to make and expectations to anticipate. We are affixed further through shared commonalities. Languages may be different but they all exist for the same purpose and that is to communicate. Clothes may be different but they are made for the covering of the body. Shoes are for the feet, books are for reading and the list continues on without end.

The point to grasp is with all the energy we employ to separate ourselves from certain parts of society, the more we become entangled because we work so hard not to be like them that we continue to accentuate their lives. And our thrust and objective is to make sure nobody thinks I am like them. The more we speak of them the larger we make them. Skill is developed through practice, but stars are mad by pundits who are able to persuade the public.

The next point to be explored is the idea that no one wants to be bored. The validation of life formed in our enjoyment of it. We are taught very early in life about making decisions that serve us in meaningful positive ways. I vividly recall as a very young man being told the importance of church, school, respect, and making wise choices. These were areas of particular interest to my parents because they had lived long enough to understand that not being bored did not mean you had to be bad. Boredom seems to rob us of enjoyment and consequently life becomes seemingly empty.

So if we are bored, we are vulnerable to welcome the bad. Boredom is almost assured when we fail to develop personal interests that do not involve anyone but ourselves. We are to understand that our lives are lived by us, and not necessarily through some other human unit. No one was ever created to keep us amused so that we would have eternal happiness at our fingertips. God created us to live. If we are not living with someone, that's okay. We must remember our life was order and fashioned by Him for us to live.

Rudolph Buttmann stated that to live is to experience authentic existence. That is to say, we should know how to feel an unencumbered life, a life that is ordered but also augmented. Ordered that our lives are based on sound values, and are engaged in the positive development of humanity, but augmented to the extent that it transcends difficulties and continues to be itself amid personal crisis. If personal crises can dictate the level of enjoyment in our lives, our lives really don't belong to us, but rather to a foreign invader who has been empowered by some unknown phenomena who can, in effect, play havoc with our psychological and emotional existence when it decides to. This invader appears without being summoned.

You have to be invited to my life's shindig. You were a minute insignificant mendicant who could do nothing but engage in a parasite endeavor designed to leave us robbed and hijacked of quality existence. It is important for all of us to review the "guess who showed up at our life's party" against the "guess whose names appear on the invited" list. Like most parties, without strict security some will crash the party and subtract much of the splendor of the moment. But parties well planned, well organized, and designed to be considered unforgettable, there is a ubiquitous presence of security. Security is in place not because you expect problems, nor because you desire problems, but in the event a problem does show up, security keeps the problem on the periphery instead of allowing it in the privacy of the premises.

Furthermore, as we study Sidotharta Gautama's journey to enlightenment, it was quite interesting what he encountered. The beginning of his quest is to understand who Siddahartha Bantam was. Religion would later call him Buddah. But before he became Buddha, he experienced a great inner struggle, one that would put him at odds with the path his father had carved and the path we would later choose. To find this enlightenment was to find life for young Siddharta. And his thirst for the waters of understanding passes through the uncharted means of possibilities for this budding great thinker.

Although his father tried vigorously to fashion his ideas and life's pattern, young Siddharta responded with an unmistakable "no". "No!" said Siddharta to the 40,000 young beautiful dancing girls who were at his beckoning. "No!" to the highness of social and political aristocracy. "No!" to a life of marriage to a beautiful woman, kissed by the lips of Gabriel, baptized in the pool of charm, and covered by the fleshy garments of gentility. "No!" he said, to the opportunity of fatherhood, which was an obvious way for the world to know you are here. "No!" to watching his seed morph from childlike naiveties to adolescent wanderings to adulthood intricacies.

He was so profound that he kissed his wife and child goodbye, and he with his unguent mounted horses and into the mystic night they rode. They rode and they rode. Their journey navigated their journey. They traveled without destination. They expected everything would happen but prepared for nothing. Minute after minute passed. And what a minute each minute must have been. A minute has only 60 seconds in it, but still a minute, unsummoned and yet it moved in the way and inferred use it or lose it but staying for another second I cannot. What you do with this minute determines regarding what options you have for the next minute? But refusing to do anything bothers not the minute; it's only up to you to decide since you're in it, you might as well win it.

To live is to understand the full impact of the moment. Because the moment is so filled with expectancy, it is left underserved unless we fill it. The moment so excited by the idea that right now somebody is about to do something. This present moment has been waiting every since time was given authority to march across the meadows of the world for its turn to grace our humanity in hopes that its moment would be one of distinction. Can you imagine lying dormant for years, watching moment after moment, escaping purgatorial existence to finally intercourse with someone who can make its entrance special and its exit unforgettable and to reach that place of opportunity and either told or shown that your coming was so insignificant that it was almost a sin that purgatory had the nerve to vomit you at all?

Your coming was the result of pain in the digestive tract of time. What an awful feeling that must be. To come to the party only to be shown that your vile presence would have been more appreciated if it existed on some other planet, with some other people, and in some other time. That is the picture, however grim we see of a moment not used wisely. It must be noted that it's just a moment that will depart as swiftly as it arrive. So remember to do something good with it, because it can never be retrieved. The rewind button only works with machines and not mortals.

What is a wisely spent moment? Is it when your face expresses the joy of laugher? Is it when you figure out some way to insulate or immune yourself from the pressures surrounding your life? Perhaps these approaches massage our emotions at last long enough for us to get through the rigors of the moment but candidly, a well spent moment is one that positively impacts the minute. It is when you do something right now that causes you to benefit perpetually. In other words, it is an act done in the present that creates benefits in the future. This is really a call for us to "invest the moment". Perhaps one of our greatest problems with our moments is the idea that enjoying the moments transcends investing the moments.

Now we certainly should not abandon the idea of enjoyment, but investing the moment usually yields greater dividends, ergo, a greater quality of life in general. For example, when we rather eat, sleep, and lounge around all day everyday our bodies become tired, lethargic, and without physical drive. And when obesity and hypertension, are the results, we are brought to the conclusion that our enjoyment becomes our investment and our return is commensurate to our commitment made to our bodies. All "investment moments" count in the larger scheme of our lives because we must remember the moment is the prelude to the minute, and short-term pleasure is usually transformed into long-term pain.

Who are you and what did the Architect have in mind when you were being considered as a potential member of a society that would aid you in understanding you? What an intricate process it must have been in the making of you. Because although human beings who functioned with great similarity as you would, each being has been created with a uniqueness that provides each some kind of distinction. What is so mind-boggling is the fact that you are united with everyone of the world and simultaneously disconnected just enough for you to explore new philosophies and shape new ideas. From the infinite cell of housed souls, God chose one that would fit and agree with the flesh house that has been carefully constructed to keep and maintain a dwelling place for the chosen soul. That would ultimately become the leveling and most influential character in the presenting yourself to the world.

Now we must consider the omnipotence of God. He was careful without being fastidious that a "freak" culminated in his creative genius. He was careful that each soul would define that you possessed the capacity to represent in some meaningful way, the Creator's enormous skill and will and that it would be on complete display in the created. He (the Creator) knew in advance which soul should occupy each body and to whom each body should be assigned in order that His creation would be balanced socially, intellectually and economically. What is so spectacular is that He achieves by allowing the created to participate in the development of the process. Then no one created can place disappointment on the Creator because although He said the poor will be with you always, He never said it had to be you.

He was saying even though I give you power to have wealth according to Deuteronomy so will choose poverty over wealth. What God was saying is that society will be balanced in every area but the corner of the worked upon which you hold is determined by what and where you place you. Socially, intellectually, emotionally, and even spiritually are behaviors you learn, and if you are determined you desire the environment that gives you the results sought by you, you allow yourself to be shaped and fashioned by them.

Academic degrees, innate brilliance, or acumens of distinction will do precious little by way of altering who you are. After you become aware of yourself, you are asked to make a call about what you consider yourself to be. Whatever the environment, whatever seems to impact, the light of the Creator never goes out. The light of escape, the pathway to new direction never before trodden are constructed the same time the obvious hidden road that leads to places where the masses eat, drink, and wallow in the defecation of human meaning. Up ahead there are warning signs, in from of you there are information signs; they are there. God made sure they are there. It is his Divine Purpose to make sure they are there so you will know that you can turn off this road and pursue the journey on the road that is virgin regarding your occupancy.

You are made by the greatest mind that to the student it would create greater human confusion, and to physically see it would be doom for the beholder. The magnificence of this mind that created you, created your world before He created you. He creates a world, then He creates you, and then tells you that its your turn to participate in the process. The Creator responded to the need to create the world, and you responded by refining and replenishing it.

Every person has pondered as they move towards adulthood the question of marriage or special interpersonal relationship. Even if you never marry formally, most people feel interconnected with someone or they would welcome "someone special" in their lives. This is normal for us to feel that way so please do not allow yourself to feel like this idea takes you out of the will of God. It is wonderful to serve a God who not only created us but completely understands that we are social beings and therefore eagerly embrace opportunities to socialize with other members of His wonderful world.

Socializing and interacting with all of society allows us to experience new cultures, and be a part of a much larger world with global influence being made and deposited in our lives. This significance on a personal level of socializing is that it creates impetus for a cascade of emotions opportunistically campaigning for the attention and interest of someone with whom desire has been inflamed. Again, this too falls in the range of normal accepted behavior. The real question regarding relationships is found in the proposition of "Who should be sought or pursued as a person of interest for me?"

Pursuant to the idea of establishing and sustaining long fulfilling relationships, I recall a message I delivered in church during the sweltering heat of August 2008. This particular Sunday morning appeared to be like so many before with perhaps one glaring difference and that was a message derived out of intense study of the first family recorded in biblical literature. You guessed it, the Adam and Eve saga.

When God made man it was an interesting creation process and product. Firstly, God showed us the infinite mind He possesses by making man with obvious hue and later man became human, a man of color. Also, if we consider the physical essence of man, we are brought into another fascinating dimension of God's omnipotence if that's at all possible.

You see, man was formed out of the dust of the ground and somehow is so packed and packaged that the torrential winds of meteorological storms have never blown our anatomies into separate particles of our original granular essence. It is as though God used an incredibly durable type of dust or clay; a kind held together by some unexplainable invisible suture with cells and pores that absorbs pain, trauma, bruises, and cuts and seemingly by the entrance of osmosis the anatomical terrain rejoins itself, closes the gaps on the skin's surface, and allows the body to maintain its standing. We must also consider the structure of this wonderful creation called "man." Without engaging in speculative anthropomorphism, was God giving us some kind of visual concept of His Being?

Just what are we to gather from the structural concept of man? Certainly, the human anatomy is a perfectly ordered mechanism, with imperfect proclivities. Does the Creation show us the absolute perfection of God's Being? Maybe God was inverting some element of His Perfect Self for us to know that he Is. God's perfection was carefully and methodically revealed with the creation of man. In Genesis 1:26, God for the first time in recorded history referenced a larger essence of Himself by saying (almost through a proposal process) let us make man. Who and where were the "us" to which he refers?

We are all abundantly aware that "us" is used in a plural sense under the conditions of which we are aware. So why all of a sudden in reading this Pentateuch book of beginnings we go from "And God said Let there be" to His saying before creating the human element, "Let us"? If God needed permission or approval to create man, does this notion of permission diminish Him in some way? Well, my friends, God was alerting us to a triune manifestation of His Presence. He was preparing us for the "us in me" understanding.

The idea of a polytheistic understanding of Him abides in the theater of obscurity, this passage undulates a more comprehensive scope of God that was germane to a certain event, or to validate a particular presence of God. For example, Jehovah-Salome, which God is peace, or Jehovah-Jireh, which is God is our provider are names of the same God manifesting Himself in varied positions of power.

Now that we are clear on the polytheistic augment or the removal of it from rational theological thinking, we can turn our attention to this thing called man. After God finished creating man, God gave him instructions. Interestingly enough, God took from man a rib to make him a help mate and to accomplish this, God had to invade man to get it. But God did not invade him until he instructed him. Wow! Isn't that amazing? Many a person struggle with the understanding of God because they expect from Him before they respect who he is. We are clearly shown that God invades us after he instructs us.

Now in Genesis 2:20, God had already created man and had given man dominion and direction. But man was not given a mate or companion until he had demonstrated a competence to lead. God was concerned about man's development before God entrusted him with the lives of others. One of the glaring assignments that Adam seemed to have mastered was the "naming of the animals". The naming of the animals was not simply and academic exercise, it was a task that required study and the employment of a carnal methodology. Adam had to study animal behavior, animal habits and their seemingly innate tendencies. And from gathering substantial data and reviewing volumous matererial, he then had to call them something that would be eternal.

Can you imagine the genius he must have had? The incredible species of birds and fish that exist seemingly without number, he called them something. Here we are able to appreciate the capabilities of the human mind. To call them something required diligence and deliberation. To stay with the task required patience and pragmatism, day in and day out, not given too much social relaxation, must immersed in this daily grind of getting them named. Those birds and fish with all these exotic colors illustrating the magnificent imagination of, God especially when he holds pastel colors of paint in His Hands and when he decided to adorn them with a kind of tropical piquancy.

Amid the creation of God, Adam called them something. He called them something that God would agree with. Adam called and God concurred (or agreed with). What an awesome entrustment for God to tell you to call something and essentially stand with is a special mantel God does not seem to give to everyone. This is evidenced in Exodus 7 when God said to Moses I will make you a god unto pharaoh and Aaron will be your prophet. This is another special moment when God did the unusual.

The establishment of marriage as seen in the Genesis text creates yet another moment for those of us with theological interests to be again dazzled by God's mental infinity. If we follow the sequence of events, we will see that Adam's mate emerged after he demonstrated management. Adam was given the task and opportunity to manage. Now failure to manager properly simply means you "mismanaged." Since I have a fetish with words and language and the images they present, let's view it this way. When man fails to manage he "mis-manages." The man misses. Now most men I know would feel offended if someone would refer to them as a "Mis" manager. I just hope from this jestful play on words that all me would "man the age"; ergo, MANAGE themselves to the extent that they bring pleasure to God.

Secondly, when God created Eve (Adam's helpmate), He, according to the Genesis account, caused Adam to enter into a deep sleep, which could be interpreted medically as a kind of anesthesia moment. It was during this time when it appears the first medical operation was performed. God carefully extracted a rib from Adam which would serve as the initial element about which He would create Eve. Which rib was used, I hear you asking? From which side might be your follow-up question? The truth is the rib number is irrelevant, and from which side is inconsequential. But what is to emerge from all of this is the fact that she was made from his ribs, and the rib protects the essential organs for life which some could now assume you should be united to the one who protects your heart. Also, the fact that God used Adam's rib reveals that God meant for her to walk beside her husband. Furthermore, the removal of Adam's rib and using it to create Eve reveals that Adam's mate was in him. God used something from Adam to create something for Adam. Is that an awesome strategy? God brought to him what was from him to ensure capability with him.

Lastly, I will leave this section with a thought over which to ponder. In Genesis 2:24, we read, "Therefore, shall a man leave his father and his mother, and shall cleave unto his wife: and they shall be one flesh." This is called the "leaving and cleaving" equation. In other words, amid the creation of Adam and Eve, we are told to leave your mother and your father and cleave unto your wife and neither Adam nor Eve could ever share in this concept because they had neither one. Just something to think about!

Chapter Eleven

The Curse Of Success

To whom much is given, much is required

These immortal words will never fade away as long as humanity continues. And as long as our world continues to exist, we will have successful individuals. There will always those who transcend the ordinary and rise to the level of extraordinary. All of us should push ourselves to reach or highest potential, because we elevate our humanity, and inspire so many coming after us to do the same. I have often said in many a sermon that each blessing comes with a burden.

Many times, we are unable to maintain the blessings that are bestowed because we have great frustration in trying to bear the burden. Early in my life, it became apparent to me to be very careful for what you ask God, because you just might get it. Further, I have discovered with this that God does sometimes grant us our request to reveal to us that our desires need to be modified to fit in our burden-bearing capacity. Because wanting something is very easy, but bearing the burden of responsibility to keep it, is altogether is another exercise. Also, as we attain the goals that render us successful, we have to remember our success is not isolated from others who either know us, or assisted us in some way to be successful.

So our success is connected with others, and whether we acknowledge it or not, no one reaches any level of success by themselves. Let us for a moment, place this idea in the African American cultural context. Many college graduates are still the first in their families to reach this accomplishment. Many parents struggled, and sacrifice to make sure their child or children could go to college because their social and financial conditions were not able to accommodate this higher learning opportunity. So many of our parents were so determined to create a better life for their children were at peace with this idea. Truthfully, I am emotionally moved, and inspired each time I hear stories like this, and these kinds of stories are not unusual, but rather typical within the black community.

In short, it means one generation sacrifices, so the next generation succeeds. Also, this idea ties together, and nurtures a much stronger bond between the generation of sacrifice, and the generation of success. This is the intent. We should tie the generations together, and therefore strengthen the bonds of love within the family unit.

I am happy I did not have to entertain the idea of not being able to go to college. The way to go to college was already in place when it was time for me to go, but this is not true at all for many Black students. Some have to immediately find a job, and earn some money because times have been very hard for the family for many years, and kids just don't want to burden the family any further than what had been done already. So to many, college was not a part of the equation.

Another interesting idea associated with this subject is how so many of our kids are born without the parents planning for the arrival of the baby. Consequently, when the child is born, parents have to do whatever is necessary for the child to live, grow, and develop. So when the child is simply the result of parental sexual exchange, it becomes increasingly difficult for parents to save money, or provide from their means any amount of money for a college fund. This became really apparent to me one day I was teaching high school economics and history class. I ask the students a question regarding their future, and out of almost no where one of the students said, "Dr. Everett, none of us in this class was really thought about before we got here. We were accidents, merely the results of our parents getting their sexual groove on!" Then it hit me. This young man's entrance into the world was not accidental, but to the parents certainly not intended.

Even amid the uncertainties regarding the entrance or arrival of our children, sober parents still sacrifice for their children in hopes that they (the children) will fare better in life then they did. So many parents in our community immersed themselves in trying to bring up the best child they can. Often the primary care for the child is the mother, who tirelessly gives and gives to make sure her child has a fair chance to escape the confines of poverty, and one day find him or herself in at least the lap of comfort. But wait a minute. Will the child be the only recipient of economic and social comfort?

Absolutely not. The sacrificing parent too is to reap some benefit because of the past struggles they endured

Now the successful child that comes from the poverty that once imprisoned them must view his success in the light of who helped him get there, and what if any responsibility he has to his parent(s)? Along with that, was about the other siblings who, for whatever reason, did not fair as well, and they, too, are connected with the success of that individual? Isn't it amazing? A family of six, seven or even eight, may have one who decides to try his luck at life differently then the rest. He or she is not placed in an unusual place. The successful ones move to another neighborhood, and run with another group who just happens t be doing similar things professionally and socially, what does he or she become to the family that is still back in the 'hood?

Transcending the ordinary to rise to the extraordinary

Many successful African Americans are like you or me. However, some factors contribute to the success of some, but others are not the recipients of these factors. But first, we must consider the varying definitions of success. Success can mean making what we consider a lot of money, attaining a dream job or climbing the ranks in our perspective fields, or attaining advanced degrees. Depending on the circumstance, attaining a high school diploma is the epitome of success if this milestone has not been achieved by others within a family. Whatever the definition of success is, they all have the common denominator of what has been an unattainable goal, especially in the black community.

All of us are born to either a single or a two parent family. Each of these scenarios can provide comfort and support needed to be successful. Whether it is a one or two parent household, parents normally have the same goal, even though the financial circumstances may be different. For example, we are most familiar with athletes who come from the confines of poverty to transcend social and economic barriers to become multimillionaires. However, we must recognize factors with the superstar athletes and the kids from the projects who all attain what we define as success.

Supportive adults in one's family are the catalyst for success. Let's consider some examples of how parents or surrogate parents can offer support. We do need to consider, however, that parents who want to insure the success of their children, have not always attained the level of success that they may have wanted or may have dreamed of. As I stated earlier, we must continue to know who is in our child's lives, from their teachers to their friends. Parents (or surrogate parents, in some situations) share mistakes that they made that caused them not to attain the level of success they may have desired years ago. For example in some households, marrying young, sometimes even in the teenage years, can divert a dream and instead, find ourselves on a path far from where we want to be. With marriage comes the responsibility of children, managing the household, or employment that takes up an exorbitant amount of time and even resources.

One generation sacrifices, and the other succeeds

Marrying young in the black family, especially during the time of segregation where opportunities were sparse, closed many doors for individuals who found themselves in a predicament that presented difficult financial, social, and emotional situations. Couples would marry as early as 14 or 15 years of age. This created a situation where, if two parents were involved, the father worked, and the mother stayed at home and managed the household and the children. If we look at this even further, this meant that the father, who was working at a job he may not have desired, worked tirelessly to insure that his family had enough on which to survive. This could mean working tireless hours at the behest of others because more times than not, the father would not be in a position to own his own business, or be in the position to support himself without working for someone else. The role of the father meant that food would be on the table, and a home would be provided for the dependents in the family.

The role of the mother, on the other hand, was quite different than that of a working father. Along with the responsibility of bearing children, which could be, at times, double-digits, the mother had a very critical role. The mother had the responsibility of preparing the food, making sure that children were clothed and fed as well as being a mother to others in the neighborhood who may not have had the love and support of a parent or caring adult. Along the way, the mother, who was present most of the time with the children, infused various lessons along the way.

One lesson that mothers often taught in the home was to respect the teacher who was delivering instruction. Now why was this important? The answer is two-fold. First, the way in which a teacher was treated was a direct reflection on the parents. In other words, if a parent was disrespectful a teacher, then surely, teachers and others would think that the same behavior was occurring in the home. This, in turn, was a poor reflection on the child and not the adult. Within this lesson, parents also seemingly indirectly taught the values of an education. Even thought the mother may not have been educated herself, she knew the value of an education and the source from which it came.

Mothers also taught other lessons to their children, which was a part of child rearing. That lesson was that an education will get you very far in life. Mothers who were not educated knew this because they recognize the condition in which they were in, and knew that perhaps there was something far better that an education could provide. Having an education meant that children would not have to toil long tireless hours at menial jobs that did nothing but provide a means to an end. Also, having an education meant that the children could find themselves in better social and economic situations.

The role of the mother and father in similar situations were very different, but both were very crucial to the development of the child. Both set examples that morals, hard work, and perseverance were bound to pay off. In many situations, the offspring did go on to graduate from high school and did not bring shame to the family by committing an act that would surely bring embarrassment to the family. Once children "make it", they have extremely enormous shoes to fill, and the benefits of their success will reach far beyond the immediate family.

In the least desirous of home situations, many still go on to graduate from high school. In some situations there are those that go on to attain advanced degrees, own his or her own business, or perhaps become a successful athlete.

Sharing the benefits of success

As stated earlier in this chapter, we are not blessed with success to uplift ourselves. This is God's ways of intending us to help others. Once we go on to become successful in our various fields or endeavors, we must remember that there are those who have helped us along the way. This could be a special aunt, a favorite uncle, an inspirational teacher, or a preacher that we have remembered growing up that has helped us along the way. We must keep in mind that help does not necessarily mean from a financial point of view. Receiving help and guidance can come from receiving hand-me-downs throughout our school years from a relative so that we do not have to go without. Attaining help can also come in the form of strict discipline we may recall from a teacher who loved us, yet gave us a good paddling when needed so that we would not make the same mistakes.

But most importantly, our parents, or surrogate families who have sacrificed tirelessly, have given in ways many of us take for granted. For at least the first 18 years of our lives, our parents have sacrificed time, money, their own education, have put aside their own dreams and aspirations, and have been there for us through the thick and the thin. Let us also remember that raising a child is not cheap; but instead the cost of raising a child comes with a high price, from countless nights up worrying where the child is, or through enduring situations where children have disappointed or embarrassed us for all of the world to see. And sometimes, we have to battle with ungrateful children who do not know or care to know the cost of the sacrifices parents have made just so that the children will have a better chance in life.

Whether acknowledged or ignored, the fact remains that children are forever indebted to the love, support, and sacrifice parents have made. The term "forever indebted" may not go over well with some of you. I am reminded of a conversation that I had with a church member some years ago. She and her husband have been married for some time. The oldest of four children, the husband had come from a single-parent home where his mother and grandmother raised him and saw that he received the best education possible. He later became very successful, and married an equally successful wife. His wife thought that whatever money came into the household, should remain in the household.

Additionally, the wife believed that what was not spent, should be saved for a "just in case" situation. I assure you. All of these things are true, when placed in the right context. However, the wife failed to realize one simple thing. It was the mother who was her husband's first love. That is not to say that he does not love his wife. Nor does this meant that the mother will be cared for and the wife will not. This also does not mean that the wife is secondary. This is to simply point out that before the husband loved his wife, he loved his mother.

It is important for us to remember that it is not taboo to mention that this husband's first love was his mother. Let us examine why this is the case. First, the mother in this situation made sacrifices that included working two, sometimes three jobs simultaneously to make sure her son could go the best private Catholic school in the city. Her son did not have to go to private Catholic school. But at the time, if it was the public school in this city that her child was to attend, her son was sure to become a statistic. Secondly, the mother went without purchasing clothes year after year for herself so that her son could have the necessities needed to be successful in school. The mother gave her son countless lessons on how to make it through school, how to interact with people, and how to be self-sufficient. Working several jobs can take a tremendous toll on one's personal well being if done year after year. The mother disciplined her son with tough love so that he would be able to withstand the pitfalls of life all while teaching him to be a better success at life than she was. All of these factors are key in becoming a successful adult in today's world.

But since the onset of their marriage, the wife could not understand why her husband would continue to financially help his mother in some form or fashion which seemed to the wife month after month, year after year. We have to consider this: The sacrifices the mother and grandmother put forth are priceless. Without them, there would be no him. Not in the physical sense, but the person that in astute enough to navigate tough situations as well as to be able to provide for a family. So I informed this member that she must look at her husband's giving not as him forsaking her. Instead, she should realize that her husband knows intimately the sacrifices that his mother had made for him while he was growing up. She must also realize that the fact that her husband assists or shows his love monetarily to his mother is not a deal breaker for their marriage, especially if it does not interfere with the orderly operations of her their home. It is simply her husband giving back to show his appreciation for his mother making him into the man that stands today.

Cursed with Success

Having created success can be a blessing. But it can also be a curse. Having the blessings of success means that one is comfortable, can attain many of the things he or she wants while remaining spiritually grounded, or having success means that we have met a milestone in a lives that we feel completes us. On the other hand, success can be seen as a curse, especially when success brings along responsibility that we are not yet equipped to handle.

As we become successful, we must remember that God did not allow us to achieve this level of success and keep it all for ourselves. We have been blessed with becoming successful so that that we can reach back and help others. We have been blessed with success so that others can see that they too may have the opportunity to be successful if they see an individual that has already been down the road and proved that success can be achieved in a successful manner. We have also been blessed with success in order for us to be examples for others to see God working in or lives.

We may also feel that we are cursed with success. Take for example a successful rapper. Some rappers feel that even though they are successful, they must remain true to "the game" by continuing to stay in "the 'hood", or continuing to be portraying themselves in a gang when in their private lives, this definitely is not the case. Additionally, a lot of rappers know that the worse thing that they can do is to appear to be a "sell out", or one who abandons their background in order to assimilate with the status quo. So we have to connect these performers who continue to fall into the trap of committing crimes such as burglaries and robberies when obviously they should be far removed from these acts based upon the level of success they achieved.

In additionally with these performers, we still see in many instances that their surroundings, or friends, do not change once a certain level of success is attained. Now I am not saying that once you "make it", you should cut everyone off and start a new life. What I am saying is that once a certain level of success is achieved, we sometimes allow those who mean us no good to hang around us and shape our lives, all the while recognizing that we do not need these people in our lives. Some people in these situations allow other people to bring them down. The harm in this is that these actions sometimes put our own success at risk, therefore threatening everything for which one has worked. Another case is the case of a famous athlete who was recently caught up in a situation that caused him to be confined to prison for some years. Now we all make mistakes. But the mistake that this athlete made was that he did not abandon his prior lifestyle or "friends" when he achieved the epitome of success for many high school athletes, and that is achieving the status of professional athlete. The high cost of success means that there is a high cost whenever the law is broken by someone in the public eye.

Such is the case also in our lives. When we become successful, we can complete many acts of kindness, generosity, and other acts of love. But when we reach a certain level of success, I assure you that one mistake will forever cloud all of the wonderful things that were done prior to that mistake.

Sometimes in the black community, there aren't many of us that may make it to a level of success where we are in the position to help others. Keep in mind the help to which I am referring to is not just for the immediate family. Sometimes, when someone "makes it out of the 'hood", it is an expectation from those left behind that the one will reach back and help all. Often times, the one who becomes successful and is able to move out of the poor neighborhoods feels obligated to help those who are left behind. The problem with that is if a successful individual continues to help everyone who asks, then he or she is placing in danger his or her own success therefore jeopardizing everything that he or she has accomplished.

Now the successful individual has a choice to make. Does he continue to help, does he isolate himself from his friends or loved ones, or does he simply say "no"? Be mindful that each of these scenarios have potentially what one may perceive as negative consequences. Some have been criticized for moving away which appears to be a way to avoid friends and families that are left behind. If someone who has achieved a level of success isolates himself, then he may be seen as turning his back on his friends, family, or loved ones. These are not easy questions to answer. However, as already discussed, it is our obligation to help those if we are able, and deciding if we are able can be an arduous task in and of itself. But we must we blessed with the knowledge of how to help others in such a way that does not cause harm to ourselves and to or families.

Sewing the Seeds of Success

Regardless of the levels of success we are able to attain, parents provide the blueprint for what we will become. I am reminded of a class I had some years ago, and I recall my professor in my class saying that parents provide about 60% of our intelligence; the other 40% is from the environment. Now it took me a while to realize the ramifications of this statement. But if we examine it further, these numbers can have a profound effect on the babies we create and bring into the world.

Now in the 21st century, we are in a generation where a lot of young people engage in the act of smoking marijuana. Now to some, smoking marijuana, or "weed" is fun, a social event, and to be honest, down right expected in some communities. But let's consider this point: Some individuals go on to smoke weed for years and years, on up into their 20s and 30s (and of course older, in some cases). However, some individuals smoke marijuana for years. This causes a problem especially when, a female of child-bearing age decides that she is ready to have children. However, the weed we have smoked for years and years is now in our system. I am a firm believer that whatever goes into our bodies stays in our bodies. This is evident in some of us who overeat and are now unhealthy and unfortunately over weight.

My point is that when we engage in such illicit behavior, we produce offspring after smoking weed or drinking for years and years. Now if what I said is true, and that is what goes into our bodies stays in our bodies, then our seed is overtaken by the weed we have smoked for years. Now the problem is that we have these children, and we are familiar with the effects that marijuana has on the human body, as adults. But our children, who are born after (and in some cases, during) parents have smoked marijuana, exhibit social and behavior issues in school. The teachers are having problems with the students in schools. School administrators are at wits end. Students are misbehaving at home. It is now time for the black community to recognize that marijuana will have a profoundly negative effect on black youth for years to come if we o not acknowledge that this problem is being passed down from generation to generation.

We must first begin by reiterating to our adults in the community that it is not alright to smoke marijuana, nor is it fine to smoke especially in front of our children. We are teaching our children that there is nothing wrong with this act. We must also stop this generational and biological curse of contaminating our young people with the toxins found in marijuana. Individuals who smoke marijuana and go on to produce children are aiding in creating generations of troubled youth; trouble that occurs in all facets of our lives. We must be a part of the solution in solving this social ill within our community.

If we want to build success within our community, we must sew the seed of success. We can set examples for those that are watching and questioning the decisions we are making in our lives. We must demonstrate that it is expected of us to reach back and help someone else who has not attained the level of success that we have attained. To be selfish is not the will of God. Finally, we must acknowledge that we are destroying generations of youth, and stymieing the success of our youth if we continue to damage our bodies with drugs (even alcohol) and pass them on to generations that may be certainly doomed to not be successful in life.

Epilogue

After reflecting over my life, I now understand that we are to be careful and make sure we don't miss the opportunity to live. Life is so brief, and we pass through corridors so swiftly that sometimes we miss the pivotal points. We do so immersed into our own ideas, and personal agendas that new opportunities pass before we recognize what has happened. Perhaps for me, the greatest turning point of my life was the day I enrolled in Laurinburg Institute to finish my high school career because I went there to play basketball but left there with my life's purpose. I discovered as a result of graduating from that school that ministry and education would ultimately order my life's steps. That was the moment when polish was applied to my mind and the light of knowledge and discipline came into full view.

It is important for young minds to be stable. Many times our youth is wasted away in believing that life is one big social event that has no end, but truthful (as we later discover) life is often difficult. And we have to face challenging moments where we are not prepared. This is probably the reason why so many of us are better at being children than we are at being an adult. Perhaps this is the result of our becoming so dependent on someone else handling our issues (i.e. parents, aunts, uncles, grandparents, etc.) that we never figure out how to manage our lives.

It certainly is the intent of this writer to help young minds to know that it's okay to be different. You can carve new paths to your destiny, and please never permit social expectations to decide who you are. Never permit jobs or circumstances to define your being. We are God's unique vessels, and each vessel was created because God wanted each of us to do something in His world to move us closer to the image and ideas of Himself. So as I close this book, never allow yourself to get depressed by human issues that are sure to come. Life was not always meant to be fair; it was meant to be experienced. Thank you Lord for this Journey called Life.

Bibliography

Anderson, N.T. (1990). *Victory over darkness.* Ventura, CA: Regal Books.

Anderson, N.T. (1990). *The Bondage Breaker.* Eugene, OR: Harvest House.

Coley, K.S. (2006). The Helmsman: Leading with courage and wisdom. *Purposeful Designs.*

Collins, P, Collins B., & Collins D. (1996). Strategies of the Kingdom—A Briefing for war. *Retrieved November 13, 2000 from www.churchlink.com.*

Collins, P, Collins B., & Collins D. (1996). Strategies of the Kingdom—The shape of the enemy. *Retrieved November 13, 2000 from www.churchlink. com.*

Collins, P, Collins B., & Collins D. (1996). Strategies of the Kingdom—God's grand strategy. *Retrieved November 13, 2000 from www.churchlink.com.*

Collins, P, Collins B., & Collins D. (1996). Strategies of the Kingdom—Rendering the enemy powerless. *Retrieved November 13, 2000 from www.churchlink. com.*

Collins, P, Collins B., & Collins D. (1996). Strategies of the Kingdom—Advancing the kingdom. *Retrieved November 13, 2000 from www.churchlink.com.*

Collins, P, Collins B., & Collins D. (1996). Strategies of the Kingdom—Engaging the enemy. *Retrieved November 13, 2000 from www.churchlink.com.*

Collins,P,CollinsB.,&CollinsD.(1996).StrategiesoftheKingdom—Disposing the enemy. *Retrieved November 13, 2000 from www.churchlink.com.*

Collins, P, Collins B., & Collins D. (1996). Developing your Strategy. *Retrieved November 13, 2000 from www.churchlink.com.*

Evans, A.T. (1998). *The battle is the Lords.* Chicago, IL: Moody Press

Jerimiah, D. and Carlson, C.C.(1995). *Invasion of other Gods: The seduction of new Age spirituality.* Dallas, TX: World Publishers.

Kehl, D.G. (1994). *The Cosmocrats: Diabolism in literature.* Newburgh, IN: Trinity Press.

Lang, Peter (2007). *Searching for Spirituality in Higher Education.* New York: Peter Lang Publishing.

LeFevre, Perry (1987). *Inside America's Christian Schools.* Macon, Georgia: Mercer University Press.

McMillian, J.A. (1997). *The Authority of the believer.* Camp Hill, PA: Christian Publications.

Prince, D. (1998). *They shall expel demons.* Grand Rapids, MI: Chosen Books.

Sherrer, Q. & Garlock, R. (1991). *A woman's guide to spiritual warfare.* Ann Arbor, MI: Servant Publications.

Wagner, C.P., & Pennoyer, D. (1990). *Wrestling with dark angels: Toward a deeper Understanding of the supernatural forces in spiritual warfare.* Ventura, CA: Regal Books.

Edwards Brothers, Inc.
Thorofare, NJ USA
September 7, 2011